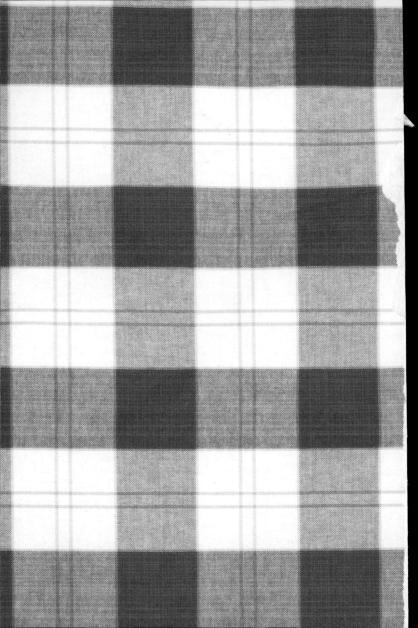

Faith

52
Breakfast
and Dinnertime
Devotions for
Families

TO

TABLE

BroadStreet
PUBLISHING

BroadStreet Publishing Group LLC
Savage, MN
Broadstreetpublishing.com

FAITH TO TABLE

© 2020 by BroadStreet Publishing®

978-1-4245-6059-2
978-1-4245-6060-8 (eBook)

Design by Chris Garborg | garborgdesign.com
Edited by Michelle Winger | literallyprecise.com

Printed in China.

20 21 22 23 24 25   7 6 5 4 3 2 1

Introduction

Spending time together around the table is critical for growing healthy family relationships. Celebrate the most connected part of your day with *Faith to Table*.

BREAKFAST TIME

- Each day begins with a morning Scripture. Have someone read the Scripture out loud.
- Next is a quick morning devotion based on the theme for the day. Read the devotion to the family.
- Ask for prayer requests. Record the requests in the space provided.
- Breakfast Time closes with a prayer for committing the day to God. Make sure you include the prayer requests in your family prayer.

DINNER TIME

- While you're at the dinner table, have someone read the evening Scripture out loud.
- Next, read the evening devotion.
- Use the "Let's Talk" questions to encourage discussion.
- Initiate a praise report by asking if anyone has experienced answers to prayers.
- Write down a few things the family is especially thankful for today.
- Use the family activity to help solidify what you have learned.
- Have someone pray the Closing Prayer and then read the "Did You Know?" paragraph out loud.

We hope you are able to use this book as a tool to impart godly wisdom for life's many challenges. Grow closer to God and to each other as you bring your faith to the table!

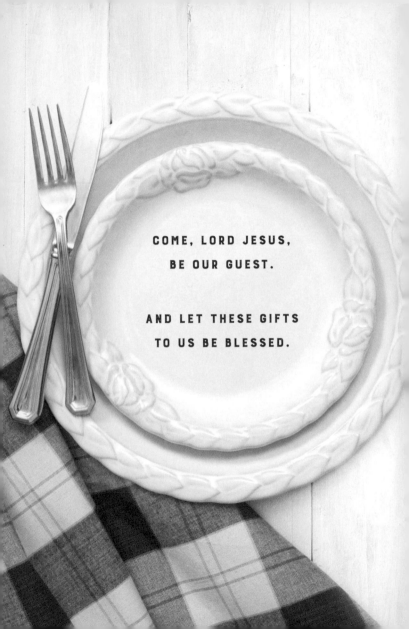

Slow to Anger

When you are angry, do not sin. And do not go on being angry all day. Do not give the devil a way to defeat you.

EPHESIANS 4:26-27 ICB

When was the last time you felt so angry you wanted to kick something or throw things around the room? It's pretty normal to feel angry about things, but you have to be careful about what you do with that anger.

What would happen if you hurt yourself, someone else, or damaged something while you were angry? It would make the situation worse, right? That's why God's Word says to find a way to calm down so you don't keep thinking about your anger. Ask Jesus to help you settle down, and then do something else like read a book, write a letter, or kick a ball around!

PRAYER REQUESTS

Dear God, sometimes we feel really mad. We know it's not good to be angry, so please help us to cool our temper when we feel it getting out of control. We want to speak less and listen more, so we can honor you better. Help us to find ways to calm down quickly when we become angry. Give us grace and patience with others today.

*You must all be quick to listen, slow to speak,
and slow to get angry. Human anger does not
produce the righteousness God desires.*

JAMES 1:19-20 NLT

Let's talk!

What things make you angry?

What helps you settle down when you are angry?

Emotions can be difficult to understand. Sometimes we think it's bad to show our feelings. That's not true. God wants us to let people know how we feel so they can join us in our emotions. He wants us to feel compassion for others and extend patience to those who make us angry.

We feel many different emotions in one day. We might go from happy to angry and back to happy in less than five minutes. It's important to understand why specific events cause certain emotions in us. We can ask God to help us control our emotions rather than letting our emotions control us.

PRAISE REPORT

Share recent answers to prayer.

What are you grateful for today?

Take turns sharing a time when you felt really angry. How did you handle the situation? Would you do anything differently next time you feel angry? Brainstorm some healthy responses to anger that you can try the next time you get angry.

Father God, thank you for your grace toward us. Help us to let go of our anger and respond in ways that demonstrate self-control and love. You are kind and forgiving, and we want to act the same way to others.

Wars can often cause a lot of destruction, but that wasn't the case when it came to the Dutch-Scilly War. Not a single life was lost during this 335-year conflict. The commander of the Dutch armies didn't feel like fighting and then everyone forgot that they were at war. In 1986, they found an old document that reminded them about the ongoing conflict, and soon thereafter a peace treaty was signed between the Dutch and the Scilly Isles, thus ending the most peaceful war in recorded history.

More than Sparrows

Give all your worries to him,
because he cares about you.
1 PETER 5:7 NCV

We can find a lot to be anxious about in a day. Will I have enough time to finish my assignment? Did I remember to feed the dog? Does my hair look ok? Do people really like me? None of these worries are too small or too big for God. He cares about all of them.

We forget just how much he cares when we focus on our problems instead of his blessings. He gives us promises like our verse today to remind us that we are his when it seems like we have a lot to be anxious about.

PRAYER REQUESTS

God, whenever we begin to feel anxious today, whether we're worried about big or small things, help us to tell you how we feel and then trust that you will take care of us. Thank you for always being near to us and providing us with your peace.

"Look at the birds of the air; they neither sow nor reap nor gather into barns, and yet your heavenly Father feeds them. Are you not of more value than they? And can any of you by worrying add a single hour to your span of life?"

MATTHEW 6:26-27 NRSV

Do you know how sparrows get their food? How do they find safe places to rest at night? God designed nature so creatures like birds don't have to worry. Sparrows find big beautiful trees to keep safe in at night, and they wake up to find their breakfast in the dirt in the morning.

God doesn't want us to be anxious either. He says that he cares even more for us than he does for the sparrows. If those little birds don't have to worry about life, then neither do we! We can trust God to take care of us.

Let's talk!

What things cause you to feel anxious?

What steps can you take to trust God through your anxiety?

PRAISE REPORT

Share recent answers to prayer.

What are you grateful for today?

Write down five things that seem to make people anxious in your family. Then list how you can help each other through those anxious moments.

Dear God, we need to learn to trust you more because you care about us and our troubles. We can be anxious about a lot of things, but we don't ever need to feel like we are alone. Help us to reach out to you the next time we are worried.

DID YOU KNOW?

Eating healthy food, getting the right amount of sleep, participating in physical exercise, and spending time doing something relaxing are all great ways to help fight anxiety. Sharing your concerns with your family and being understanding of each other can go a long way to helping those in the family who might struggle with anxiety.

A Long List

My God will meet all your needs.
He will meet them in keeping with his
wonderful riches. These riches come to you
because you belong to Christ Jesus.
PHILIPPIANS 4:19 NIRV

When your mom or dad makes a shopping list, they go around looking for any food that might be running out that the family will need.

God is always checking to see what we need. He gives us what we need and then he gives us extra things—we call these blessings! Blessings could be good health, kind friends, and a happy family, and they are all from God. God shows us that he cares by taking care of our needs.

PRAYER REQUESTS

Jesus, thank you that you give us all that we need, and often bless us with more! Help us to use the blessings in our lives to honor you today.

"Even more blessed are all who hear the word of God and put it into practice."
LUKE 11:28 NLT

Let's talk!

What gifts has God blessed you with lately?

What needs has God taken care of for you this week?

Count your blessings. That might be something you hear a lot, but do you know what it means? Every good thing in our lives is a blessing from God. Think of every good thing you possibly can.

Maybe today is hard. Maybe you feel like there are more bad things than good. It's okay. Just start counting your blessings anyway. You might be surprised by how many there are!

PRAISE REPORT
Share recent answers to prayer.

What are you grateful for today?

Have each person write down five blessings God has given them. Go around the table sharing and thanking God for each blessing.

Dear God, thank you for everything you have given us. We have happy hearts when we think about all the blessings you have provided for us to enjoy. We want to use the blessings in our lives to bless others. Please show us how we can do that.

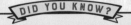

DID YOU KNOW?

Saying "bless you" is a common response in America after a person sneezes. In Germany, a response to a sneeze may be *gesundheit* which means *health*. Different countries have different responses to sneezing—make sure you do your research before traveling!

Continue Strong

*"Remember that I commanded you to be strong
and brave. So don't be afraid. The Lord your
God will be with you everywhere you go."*

JOSHUA 1:9 ICB

What does it feel like to stand up in front of a class to read something out loud or talk to a group of people about a project you just finished? Do you get a little nervous? Do you get really nervous? Don't worry, many people are not comfortable talking in front of a large group.

The next time we face something that makes us nervous, we can remember that we have a big strong God standing right next to us. He can give us the courage to do anything. We can take a deep breath and relax! God is on our side.

PRAYER REQUESTS

God, please help us to overcome our fears by remembering that you are always with us. Thank you for the courage you give us. We need your strength to help us get through every challenging moment we face.

*Be alert. Continue strong in the faith. Have
courage, and be strong. Do everything in love.*

1 CORINTHIANS 16:13-14 NCV

We all need courage. It doesn't matter
if we're young or old, tall or short,
confident or shy. We could need courage
to say sorry, to perform a song, or to
stand up for what is right. We need
courage in the most boring parts of life
and in the most exciting parts.

Whatever we do, we don't have to be
afraid because God is with us. We can
be brave because we know that he helps
us with everything and he is right by
our side, all the time.

Let's talk!

When was
the last time
you showed
courage?

What do
you need
courage for
right now?

PRAISE REPORT
Share recent answers to prayer.

*What are
you grateful
for today?*

Have everyone write down one thing they need courage for this week. Remember to pray for each request and come back to this page later to see how God answered your prayers.

Dear God, you command us in your Word to always have courage. With you, we will not be discouraged or afraid. Thank you for being with us wherever we go.

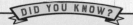
DID YOU KNOW?

Glossophobia is the fear of public speaking. It is suggested that maybe even as high as 75% of all people are afraid of getting up in front of a group of people to talk. If this is true, it would make glossophobia the world's number one fear!

Interest in Others

*Do not be interested only in your own life, but
be interested in the lives of others.*

Philippians 2:4 NCV

There were a lot of people that needed help when Jesus
was on earth. People wanted to be healed from sickness
and poor people needed food to survive. Jesus didn't
forget about the people that were doing the right thing
either. He knew that life could be hard for those who
were following him.

Are there ways that we can be like Jesus? Can we find
someone who is sick to pray for? Can we give something
to someone who doesn't have much? There are a lot
of people that need help in our world, and we have
something very special to give them—the love of Jesus.

PRAYER REQUESTS

*Jesus, thank you for caring for everybody. Help us to see
the needs in our world and to help where we can.*

If anyone has material possessions and sees a brother or sister in need but has no pity on them, how can the love of God be in that person? Dear children, let us not love with words or speech but with actions and in truth.

1 JOHN 3:17-18 NIV

Let's talk!

How can you care for someone in need today?

How do you like to be cared for?

We throw away things that are old, dirty, or broken because we want something new. God sees things differently. He is sad that some people are poor and hungry, and he reaches out to help them. One of the ways he helps those people is by asking us to care for them.

If you do everything you can for those in need, your light will shine through the darkness. As we help others, God helps us.

PRAISE REPORT

Share recent answers to prayer.

What are you grateful for today?

Take a moment to think about the people at your church. Is there anyone sick who you could pray for? Do you know of any families who need practical help? Pray together as a family right now for those in need.

Dear God, we care about our family and our friends. Help us to be loving and caring like you are, and not to think only about ourselves. Show us how we can best care for those around us this week.

DID YOU KNOW?

During the 1800s the United States was engaged in a civil war. Thousands of women served as nurses to the wounded soldiers on the battlefield. But these women were not like nurses we know today; they were simply caring women who sacrificed their time and energy for the many hurting men. Clara Barton is the most well-known Civil War Nurse because she went on to form the first chapter of the Red Cross in the United States. But she wasn't a trained nurse either. She had a few years of simple experience caring for sick family members before she dedicated her life to caring for dying soldiers.

Unchanging

Trust in the LORD forever,
for the LORD, the LORD himself,
is the Rock eternal.
ISAIAH 26:4 NIV

When people talk about the person they trust the most, they might describe that person as being their rock. A rock put in a box for many years will look exactly the same on the day the box is re-opened. Rocks don't change.

The same goes for God. He does not change. He is always present, always caring, always delighted to spend time with us. If we choose to pray every day, or we only remember to pray at church, he doesn't ignore us. He listens every time. We can always count on God to be faithful and good.

PRAYER REQUESTS

God, you are our rock. We can trust you with our lives because we know you will never take back your promises, and you are always good. You are steady and unchanging. Thank you that we can cling to you when everything else is changing around us.

*Jesus Christ is the same
yesterday and today and forever.*

HEBREWS 13:8 NIRV

What is the biggest rock that you have seen? Did you try to pick it up? How heavy do you think it was? Rocks are strong and secure and the biggest ones are almost impossible to move.

When we start to worry, or become afraid, we can think about God like a rock. No matter what it is we are going through, he won't move. He will stay strong and steady right beside us. He is bigger than any of our troubles or fears. We can always trust him!

Let's talk!

What kind of changes do you want to make for Jesus?

How does it make you feel to know that God does not change?

PRAISE REPORT
Share recent answers to prayer.

What are you grateful for today?

It's time to get out those old family photo albums. Show your children pictures of when you were young and when they were babies. After discussing how much everyone has changed over the years, recognize that God never changes; he is the same yesterday, today, and forever.

God, change can be scary, like moving to a new house or going to a new school. But changing for you means being kind and generous and helpful to our friends and family. We want to make that kind of change. Thank you that you are perfect and you never change!

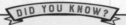
DID YOU KNOW?

The Mimic Octopus is fascinating to watch due to the fact that they act like many other animals. For example, they may move along in the water mimicking the slithering of an eel. They have been observed mimicking plenty of other animals too, including stingrays, jellyfish, and starfish. Not only do they copy the movements, but they also turn their bodies different colors so they will fit the description well.

Finding Confidence

BREAKFAST TIME

I can do everything through Christ,
who gives me strength.

PHILIPPIANS 4:13 NLT

There are very few people who have the natural gift of confidence. Most of us struggle with different areas of our lives, often believing that everyone else is probably better at everything than we are.

The only way we can feel truly confident is if we can grasp hold of what God thinks about us. When we know that his ways are perfect, his plans for us are good, and his promises are true, that's when we become bold and secure.

PRAYER REQUESTS

God, thank you for your promises that are good and true and right. We can be confident in your love for us. Help us to show others where they can find their confidence too.

Be my rock of refuge,
to which I can always go;
give the command to save me,
for you are my rock and my fortress....
You have been my hope, Sovereign LORD,
my confidence since my youth.

PSALM 71:3, 5 NIV

Let's talk!

Describe a time when God helped you feel more confident.

What are you confident about?

When you don't know how to do something at work or school, what do you do? You can't just sit there and wait for someone to tell you. You have to go find somebody who knows and ask them for help. Most people are happy to help when you tell them you don't quite understand something.

God is the same! It gives him joy to be able to help us when we need it, because he loves us and he wants what is best for us. Let's be brave and ask him for help today.

PRAISE REPORT
Share recent answers to prayer.

What are you grateful for today?

We can be confident because of the many promises that God makes to us in the Bible. Make a list of all the promises of God that you can think of. Copy the list and post it on the fridge. For the next week whenever you open the fridge, read one of the promises out loud to increase your confidence.

Dear God, we don't always feel confident enough to talk to new people or answer questions in large groups, but we know you are there for us. You give us the confidence we need. Thank you for being our strength.

DID YOU KNOW?

It takes a great deal of confidence to become the President of the United States, and perhaps no one is a better example of this than Abraham Lincoln. Before he became the man you see on the five-dollar bill, Abe had lost eight elections, had two businesses fail miserably, and even experienced a nervous breakdown! However, he remained confident in the face of such difficulty and eventually succeeded in becoming the 16th President of the United States.

All Together

*There is neither Jew nor Gentile, neither slave
nor free, nor is there male and female, for you
are all one in Christ Jesus.*

GALATIANS 3:28 NIV

Do you ever have to divide a group of people into
smaller groups? Sometimes it's hard to choose who is
going to be on which side.

The Bible says that we are all part of God's big family.
We need to make sure we include everyone who is in this
group. God doesn't want us to be separated; he wants us
all to be together!

PRAYER REQUESTS

*Jesus, help us to see your people as part of one big family.
We want to all get along and love each other well, so
we can please you and show others that your family is
something everyone should want to be a part of.*

*Make me truly happy by agreeing
wholeheartedly with each other, loving one
another, and working together with
one mind and purpose.*

PHILIPPIANS 2:2 NLT

God's people are all part of one body. This Scripture says that God makes the whole body fit together perfectly, with each part doing its own special work. The great thing about this is that one person doesn't have to do everything! The sooner we can discover what we are really good at, and what we aren't, the better.

When we team up with people who are good at things we aren't and not good at things we are, we become a healthy body and we help each other grow. It's not always easy to get along with others, especially when we are so different, but it is rewarding when everyone works together to get a project done.

Let's talk!

Was there a time this week when you could have cooperated better?

How easy is it for you to cooperate with others?

PRAISE REPORT
Share recent answers to prayer.

What are you grateful for today?

Link arms with each other and form a circle. Try moving throughout the house without letting go. You will discover that unity works better when people communicate and help each other.

Dear God, cooperation means using others' ideas and our own to get something done. Sometimes we fight when we don't agree. Help us to be loving and understanding, so we can work better with my family, friends, and coworkers.

DID YOU KNOW?

Gladys Aylward believed that the people of China were part of God's family and they needed her help. So she went to China as a missionary in the 1930s to spread the love of Jesus. Soon after she arrived, war broke out and she ended up saving the lives of over 100 orphans by marching them through the mountains. It wasn't easy, but the older children helped the younger children and eventually they made it out the other side to safety. Gladys knew that they had to work together to survive, and she was right!

A Little Courtesy

Carry one another's heavy loads.
If you do, you will fulfill the law of Christ.
GALATIANS 6:2 NIRV

Have you ever had to move something that was too heavy to push on your own? You might have needed a friend to come alongside you and help you push it. We all need a little help sometimes.

Do you have a friend that could use a hug, or some kind words today? Be a good friend and help because Jesus wants you to show love to others.

PRAYER REQUESTS

Jesus, help us to show love to those around us today. Let us make known how much they are valued by us and by you. Thank you for the people we will come into contact with today. Help us to be courteous and kind in all we do.

Remember to welcome strangers, because some who have done this have welcomed angels without knowing it.

HEBREWS 13:2 NCV

Let's talk!

What does it mean to you to be courteous?

Can you think of an example of how you could show courtesy to a friend?

Little things are important. Offer a smile to a classmate or coworker who isn't nice to you. Say a prayer for a friend who is having a bad day. Help someone who is complaining. These little acts of helpfulness can change a person's day.

There is a reason the Holy Spirit points people out around us. Our smiles might be the first they have gotten in a long time. We can choose to give them a look of love that will bring joy to their heart.

PRAISE REPORT

Share recent answers to prayer.

What are you grateful for today?

Tonight, practice courtesy at the dinner table. Ask politely to have a dish passed (don't just reach across the table), let everyone have a chance to speak without interrupting and remember to say please and thank you. Discuss how courtesy can be shown in other situations like at school, church, work, and at the park.

Dear God, we want to build others up and make them feel good. Help us to encourage our friends and think about them before ourselves. We pray also that we would be kind to strangers and help whoever is in need.

DID YOU KNOW?

Because showing courtesy is so important, March 21st is known, among other things, as Common Courtesy Day. Although it's important to be courteous every day, this day is meant to bring awareness to the kind gestures and polite manners we should all practice. Mark this day on the calendar and be extra courteous!

A Masterpiece

BREAKFAST TIME

LORD, you have made many things;
with your wisdom you made them all.
The earth is full of your riches.

PSALM 104:24 NCV

Sometimes we get jealous of the famous actors and rock stars on TV, YouTube, or magazine covers. There are days when we want to be as good looking or popular as they are.

God did not create us to be like everyone else. He made us special. What we are good at, others might not be. We shouldn't look at what other people are good at and feel bad about ourselves. Instead, we should celebrate how wonderfully different God made us!

PRAYER REQUESTS

God, thank you for reminding us of how different and special you created us to be. We are so thankful that you are a creative God and we can enjoy each other's gifts and talents. Help us to notice your creativity today and celebrate our differences.

We are God's masterpiece. He has created us anew in Christ Jesus so we can do good things he planned for us long ago.

Psalm 104:24 NCV

There is beauty all around us. Whether the skies are blue or filled with clouds, we can marvel at how everything was formed. Trees stand tall with branches reaching to the sky, flowers bloom with beautiful fragrance, and animals scamper through forests and into burrows.

Do you ever take a moment to thank God for his amazing creation? The Bible says that the world is full of examples that prove God is real. If you haven't done it already, start looking for the beauty in God's world and thank him for it.

Let's talk!

What are your most creative gifts?

How can you use your creativity for God?

PRAISE REPORT

Share recent answers to prayer.

What are you grateful for today?

Create a work of art as a family! First, have each person choose a different colored marker or crayon. Then pass this book around the table and have each person add their contribution to the masterpiece. When the artistic juices stop flowing, take turns interpreting your creation.

Dear God, you are such a wonderful artist. You created all the awesome colors and all the different faces in this world. Help us to be creative and start using the gifts you've given us to glorify you and bring joy to others.

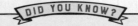

DID YOU KNOW?

Some masterpieces take longer to create than others. Mt. Rushmore took 14 years to create, and it took the Egyptians almost 30 years to build some of the pyramids. Amazingly, God created everything in the heavens and the earth in a mere six days. He truly is the greatest creator of all!

Never Give Up

BREAKFAST TIME

*We can rejoice, too, when we run into problems
and trials, for we know that they are good
for us—they help us learn to be patient. And
patience develops strength of character in us
and helps us trust God more each time
we use it until finally our hope and faith
are strong and steady.*

ROMANS 5:3-4 TLB

When you are running a relay race, you have to pass a baton to the next person before they can start running their part of the race. If you are waiting for the baton, you cheer your team on, telling the runner to keep going and not to give up.

The Bible says that we shouldn't give up on doing good. When we always try to do the right thing, we will become better and quicker at doing right. Don't quit; keep going!

PRAYER REQUESTS

Father, we don't want to give up. Help us to keep going for you. Give us the strength we need to press on when things are difficult and we don't have the energy or motivation to move forward by ourselves. We want to be determined to keep loving you and loving others.

*I have fought the good fight, I have finished
the race, I have kept the faith.*

2 TIMOTHY 4:7 NCV

Let's talk!

What does determination mean to you?

How does staying determined and winning for God make you feel?

When you have run a really long race, you usually get very tired. Sometimes you might have to stop to walk when you are feeling like you just can't keep going.

Following God isn't always easy. In fact, he tells us that the road can be difficult. But living for him is worth every last ounce of our energy. Others might be quick to tell us that it's not worth it, but Jesus says to carry on. Be strong. Keep going. Don't give up.

PRAISE REPORT

Share recent answers to prayer.

What are you grateful for today?

Describe a time when you got frustrated and wanted to give up something. Maybe it was a game you were losing, a project you couldn't figure out how to complete, or a math problem you got stuck on. What did you do? Did you give up and quit or did you show determination to keep going?

Dear God, you want us to keep trying with everything we have to finish the race and win the prize. We want to win because living forever in heaven with you is our prize. Help us to make it to the finish line with you.

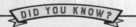

DID YOU KNOW?

It takes a lot of determination to start and finish a marathon, which is 26.2-mile race ran on foot. The worlds oldest annual marathon is the Boston Marathon established in 1897 and held every year on Patriots' Day.

A Great Reward

In all the work you are doing, work the best you can. Work as if you were working for the Lord, not for men. Remember that you will receive your reward from the Lord, which he promised to his people. You are serving the Lord Christ.

COLOSSIANS 3:23-24 ICB

Most of us have to work. Students do homework, children do chores, and adults work to take care of the bills. Sometimes jobs can be fun, and sometimes they can be boring or stressful! The Bible says to remember that we do our jobs for God, not just for others.

God loves us so much and we are promised a great reward if we work hard. If we can learn to think about our different types of work as jobs given to us by God, we will be surprised how much it helps our attitude toward our work.

PRAYER REQUESTS

God, we want to serve you. We are excited to receive the reward you have waiting for us. Help us to work with our whole hearts today, knowing we are pleasing you.

The plans of the diligent lead to profit
as surely as haste leads to poverty.
PROVERBS 21:5 NIV

Working hard can actually make you feel really good.
When you get a job done, you feel like you have done
something helpful.

Sometimes when you are asked to do a
job around the house, do you complain?
You might take a long time to do the
job. You might wish you were doing
something else. The Bible says that you
will be rewarded if you have a good
attitude about doing work. Can you
change your heart about doing jobs
others have asked you to do? If you
choose to be thankful, you might find
that you begin enjoying the work!

Let's talk!

**What would
help you
become more
enthusiastic
about work?**

**What are you
most diligent
about?**

PRAISE REPORT
Share recent answers to prayer.

*What are
you grateful
for today?*

Look at the person on your right. Do you know what kind of work they have to do? Take turns asking each other about the jobs you do. Write the jobs down then list the reward for doing the job. Thank each other for your hard work and be reminded of the reward that is coming.

Dear God, chores and work are not always fun. You say to work with enthusiasm and to work as if we are working for you. Help us to be more diligent and to have a better attitude about working.

DID YOU KNOW?

There's a reason we say "busy as a beaver." Beavers begin preparing their winter homes late in the summer and work hard through the fall to make sure everything is ready. They spend months gathering wood by chipping away at tree trunks with their teeth! That seems like a lot of hard work.

Cheerleaders

BREAKFAST TIME

Encourage one another daily,
as long as it is called "Today".
HEBREWS 3:13 NIV

Even people in the Bible felt sad sometimes. It's okay to feel upset, and it's okay to say that we are sad. Maybe a friend was unkind, or a family member, teacher, or boss yelled at us, or we were left out of a game. Maybe we didn't play well at a sports practice this week.

We should never give up! God knows when we are upset and he cares when we feel bad. When we are discouraged, it's time to ask God to speak to us. What will he say? He will say that he loves us, and he will encourage us to carry on.

PRAYER REQUESTS

Dear God, in those times we are most upset, help us to ask you for your words of truth. Thank you that you will encourage us with your love and comfort when we are sad.

Be joyful. Grow to maturity. Encourage each
other. Live in harmony and peace. Then the God
of love and peace will be with you.

2 CORINTHIANS 13:11 NLT

Let's talk!

**What
encourages
you most when
you feel down?**

**Who can you
encourage
this week?**

What does the team mascot look like for your favorite sports team? Do they have one? Do you know what it is? A mascot is someone dressed up like a character, and they are there to cheer on the sports team to encourage them to win.

Good friends take the time to cheer each other on. They show up when their friends need them, and they say kind, thoughtful things. We should be thankful for those friends in our lives, and make sure we are good friends to them too!

PRAISE REPORT

Share recent answers to prayer.

What are
you grateful
for today?

Take turns speaking an encouraging word to the person on your right. Try to be creative and lean on God's promises in the Bible for ideas. For example, "God will renew your strength" (Isaiah 40:31). "God is always with you" (Joshua 1:9). Write down the encouraging words so you can remember them throughout the week.

Dear God, it is true that kind words feel good and make the day better. Thank you for that reminder. Help us to encourage our friends and family like you encourage us.

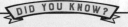

DID YOU KNOW?

Geese fly in a "V" formation to help break the wind resistance, making it easier for the group to fly. They take turns being in the front and back, giving each a break from the hard work of leading the pack. Geese will honk to encourage one another and if a goose gets hurt or sick, other geese will not leave its side until it heals.

A Better Place

A single day in your courtyards is better
than a thousand anywhere else.
I would rather guard the door of
the house of my God
than live in the tents of sinful people.

Psalm 84:10 NIRV

Imagine you are standing in the middle of two camps. On one side is a whole lot of little tents, only big enough to fit one or two people. On the other side is a beautiful huge castle, big enough to fit thousands. Where would you rather be? In the tents or at the door of the castle?

The writer of this verse said he would rather be at the door of God's great house than anywhere else. Don't you agree?

PRAYER REQUESTS

Father, thank you that you are preparing a place for us to be with you forever. Help us to remember that being with you is more important than anything else in life.

*Surely your goodness and love will be
with me all my life,
and I will live in the house of the Lord forever.*

PSALM 23:6 NCV

Have you ever been losing a game and then someone says that they would like to start over? It's like you've been given a second chance to win.

Jesus died on the cross, but then he rose again, which means he came back to life! Jesus did this to show us that even though we will die one day, we will also live again, just like he did. Don't be afraid, you have been given eternal life!

Let's talk!

What questions do you have about eternity and heaven?

What do you think of when you hear about eternity?

PRAISE REPORT
Share recent answers to prayer.

What are you grateful for today?

What do you think God's house looks like? Is it filled with gold and jewels? Are there many rooms? Draw a picture together of God's house. Be sure to include everyone's ideas to complete your masterpiece.

Dear Jesus, living forever is hard to imagine. It's kind of scary to think about sometimes. But living forever with you is exciting. Help us to understand what eternity means and how great a gift it is.

DID YOU KNOW?

Have you heard of the Eternal Flame in the Arlington Cemetery? It was lit by Jackie Kennedy to honor her husband, President John F. Kennedy after his assassination in 1963. Around the world there are many such eternal flames lit to honor countries and often the soldiers that fought for them. We even see record in the Bible of the priests being commanded to keep a continual fire burning on the altar before the Lord. Even though these flames might be considered "eternal," they pale in comparison to God's interpretation of eternity.

Simple Faith

*You love him even though you have never seen
him; though not seeing him, you trust him; and
even now you are happy with the inexpressible
joy that comes from heaven itself. And your
further reward for trusting him will be the
salvation of your souls.*

1 Peter 1:8-9 TLB

It can be difficult to believe in God because we cannot
see him. We like having our friends and family close
because they give us hugs, and we can see their faces
when we talk to them.

When God created Adam and Eve, they could walk with
him in the Garden of Eden. Now because of sin, we can
no longer look at God's face directly, but he still walks
with us. God is close to us even when we don't know that
he is. This is why we can love and trust him even though
we cannot see him.

PRAYER REQUESTS

*God, we know you are real even though we cannot see you
with our eyes. Thank you for always being with us. Help
us to listen to you as you lead us through the obstacles
in our lives.*

"Because your faith is much too small. What I'm about to tell you is true. If you have faith as small as a mustard seed, it is enough. You can say to this mountain, 'Move from here to there.' And it will move. Nothing will be impossible for you."

MATTHEW 17:20 NIRV

Let's talk!

What gives you faith in Jesus?

Do you think you have a lot of faith or a little?

Sometimes life is hard to understand. But faith is simple. When we put our faith in Jesus, God sees the goodness of Jesus in our lives, not our sin. This is how God is able to forgive us.

When troubles seem overwhelming, we can run straight to God. He gave us the gift of Jesus and everything has been made right.

PRAISE REPORT
Share recent answers to prayer.

What are you grateful for today?

Set up a few obstacles in your living room and then blindfold one family member. Designate someone else to be their guide. Using only their ears to listen to the guide, see which one of you can get from one end of the room to the other with the least amount of bumps!

Dear God, faith is a confusing thing. It's not something we can see or touch or hear, but it is trusting you in our hearts. We know Jesus died for us so we could live with you in heaven one day. Please live in our hearts today. We want you to be with us always.

DID YOU KNOW?

Jesus tells us in the Bible that if we have faith the size of a mustard seed we can do some pretty amazing things. Mustard seeds are incredibly small, measuring only one to two millimeters in diameter which is about the size of the tip of a pencil. However, some mustard plants can grow up to nine feet tall. It is the third most used spice after salt and pepper and has been around a very long time. Some seeds were found in a Chinese jar that is thought to be 5000 years old!

Better Together

Two people are better off than one, for they can help each other succeed. If one person falls, the other can reach out and help. But someone who falls alone is in real trouble. Likewise, two people lying close together can keep each other warm. But how can one be warm alone?

ECCLESIASTES 4:9-11 NLT

Have you ever been so cold that you have snuck into your parents' room to snuggle up in their warm bed? If no one was in that bed, it wouldn't be warm, would it?

God knows that people need each other; that's why he made so many of us and why he gives us family and friends. When you find people that you trust, remember to be kind and helpful to them, and make sure you ask them for help when you need it too. God created us to be in relationship with each other.

PRAYER REQUESTS

Jesus, thank you for family and friends that we can be in relationship with. Help us to love each other by being honest, caring, helpful, and generous today.

As we have opportunity, let us do good to all people, especially to those who belong to the family of believers.

GALATIANS 6:10 NIV

Families are a very important part of our lives. They are all different and special. God placed you in your family for a reason. He gave you the people you live with to love you and to help you. And he put you there to love and help them too.

You might look like other people in your family, or you might look totally different. You may be interested in music and they are interested in sports. The most important thing is that you all love and help each other.

Let's talk!

What do you love about the family God has put you in?

How is your family different than other families?

PRAISE REPORT
Share recent answers to prayer.

What are you grateful for today?

Solitaire may be a good way to pass time but it's definitely not as fun as playing a game with friends and family. Take some time tonight to enjoy each other as a family while playing your favorite card or board game. Write a list of things you each enjoy about the family you have been placed in.

Dear God, if your family is anything like ours, it's crazy but awesome. Thank you for making us part of your family so we can be surrounded by people who love you and love each other.

DID YOU KNOW?

Often portrayed as tricksters and con artists in popular folklore, wolves have a family life that is more loyal and pious than most human relationships. Normally, packs are made up of a male, female, and their offspring—making wolf packs like a family. The older offspring even help take care of their younger siblings. Sounds like wolves are better off together too.

Facing Fear

Don't worry, because I am with you.
Don't be afraid, because I am your God.
I will make you strong and will help you.
I will support you with my right hand
that saves you.

ISAIAH 41:10 ICB

Is there something you are worried about that is making it hard for you to feel okay about things? God tells us we don't need to be afraid. He will strengthen us and help us. He holds us in his hands.

Think of a steep path that goes around and up a huge cliff. Imagine yourself walking on it. You might think that you could fall. Picture God standing right next to you, holding you up. He's not going to let you fall, and he'll give you strength to take another step. It's his promise to you!

PRAYER REQUESTS

God, we don't have to be afraid because you are holding us, keeping us safe when life throws things our way. Thank you for being near to us. Help us to rest in your safe arms today.

God gave us his Spirit. And the Spirit doesn't make us weak and fearful. Instead, the Spirit gives us power and love. He helps us control ourselves.

2 TIMOTHY 1:7 NIRV

Let's talk!

What are you most afraid of?

What fears can you give to God right now?

Everyone has something they are afraid of. It might be the imaginary monster under the bed, or a fear of not making any friends. Adults are afraid sometimes too.

It doesn't matter who you are, Jesus' love is still stronger than fear. Don't be afraid because his love is perfect. His love does not punish you or hurt you. His love gives you peace.

PRAISE REPORT

Share recent answers to prayer.

What are you grateful for today?

Practice trust falls tonight! Have each child take turns closing their eyes and falling backwards into the arms of a parent. Remind each other that even when we feel like we're falling, God is always there to catch us.

Dear God, thank you for giving us a spirit of power and love. That makes us feel so safe. When we do feel afraid, help us to trust in you. With you in our lives, we have no one to fear.

DID YOU KNOW?

Jim Elliot was a missionary in the 1950s who desired to share the love of Christ with the Waodani tribe in Ecuador. Unfortunately, due to a misunderstanding, he and his four friends were killed by the very people he was trying to help. You would think that everyone would be afraid to continue working with this tribe, but his wife Elisabeth wasn't. She bravely returned to the Waodani people just two years after her husband was killed and was able to successfully bring the Gospel with her.

Already Forgiven

BREAKFAST TIME

*I will forgive their wickedness
and will remember their sins no more.*
HEBREWS 8:12 NIV

It is so hard to forget the mean things people do to us.
We tend to hold on to the hurt and the pain, but that's
not what God does. He has a loving heart that forgives.
When we say sorry, he makes us clean, as if we did
nothing wrong to begin with. He doesn't keep a list of
our mistakes. It's like they just disappear.

God doesn't remember our sin, so we don't have to
feel guilty or punish ourselves once we've asked for
forgiveness either. Isn't this a fantastic promise?

PRAYER REQUESTS

*God, thank you for forgiving us for all the wrong things
that we do. Not only do you forgive us, but you don't keep
bringing up our faults and sins when we come to you.
You forgive and forget. Help us to be more like that with
ourselves and with others.*

*God is faithful and fair. If we confess our sins,
he will forgive our sins. He will forgive
every wrong thing we have done.
He will make us pure.*

1 JOHN 1:9 NIRV

Have you ever messed something up when you were writing? What did you do? Sometimes even after you erase a mistake, you can still see faint lines on the paper where the mistake was made. Or maybe you were using a pen and you had to try another way to cover up the error—but you still know where the mistake was made.

When we sin, sometimes we think about it over and over again. We remind ourselves of how bad we were and continue to feel ashamed. God's forgiveness works better than an eraser. When we tell him we're sorry for our sin, he takes it away and cleans it up so we don't have to keep remembering it. Trust that God has forgiven you today and choose to forgive your own mistakes as well.

Let's talk!

How hard is it for you to forgive people when they are unkind?

How can you choose forgiveness even when you don't feel like it?

PRAISE REPORT
Share recent answers to prayer.

What are you grateful for today?

Do we keep a list of the way people sin against us? Have each family member use a pencil to write down a time when someone did something that hurt their feelings. Then pray that God forgives each person responsible for the situation on the list, and after you address each situation, erase it from the list. God doesn't keep lists and neither should we!

Dear God, it's not always easy to forgive others. Sometimes people are unkind to us, and we don't feel like making peace. Please help us to forgive others just as you forgave us. We want to show people your love and forgiveness.

DID YOU KNOW?

Louis Zamperini was one of many brave soldiers who ended up being captured by the enemy in World War II. He was starved and tortured for two years by the people he saw as his enemies. Eventually Louis was released, and do you know what he did? He forgave the men who treated him so horribly. He realized that if Jesus could forgive him, then he had to forgive others. Louis decided to return to the place where he was imprisoned and by the power of Jesus' love, he was able to embrace the very men who had tortured him.

Good Friends

A friend loves you all the time,
and a brother helps in time of trouble.
PROVERBS 17:17 NCV

Sometimes all we want is to be with a good friend. We want to share our joys and worries with someone who really cares. We want to enjoy just hanging out. Everyone needs friends like that.

Just like you need a good friend, so do other people. Are you being a good friend? God wants you to stick close to your good friends, to care for them and defend them. God made friendship for our good. Let's be grateful for our friends today.

PRAYER REQUESTS

God, we are so thankful for good friendships. Bless all the people in our lives who we call friends today. Help us to be good friends in return.

*There are "friends" who destroy each other,
but a real friend sticks closer than a brother.*

PROVERBS 18:24 NLT

Let's talk!

**Who are your
favorite people
to be with?**

**What friend
can you pray
for right now?**

Friends are a very important part of our lives. Some friends we keep for many years, and others we have for only a short time. Making friends is easy for some people but it's hard for others. When you find someone who shares a lot of the same values as you do, you should hold on to them and try to grow your friendship.

Friends play together, talk about life together, laugh together, and cry together. When we truly love our friends, we choose to believe the best about them, and we work to make the friendship last. God gave us a huge gift when he gave us friends. We should remember to thank him for that daily!

PRAISE REPORT
Share recent answers to prayer.

*What are
you grateful
for today?*

Take turns sharing about a time that someone was a good friend to you. How did it make you feel? Discuss ideas about how you can be a good friend to those around you this week.

Dear God, we love our friends, but we don't always show them that. Appreciating people can be difficult sometimes, but we thank you for your example of how to encourage people. Help us to show our friends that they are a blessing.

DID YOU KNOW?

Some animals have friends that don't look anything like them! Chimpanzees, elephants, baboons, horses, hyenas, dolphins, and bats have all been known to choose BFFs from other species. Maybe it's not always true that "birds of a feather flock together."

Give Generously

Tell them to use their money to do good. They should be rich in good works and generous to those in need, always being ready to share with others. By doing this they will be storing up their treasure as a good foundation for the future so that they may experience true life.

1 TIMOTHY 6:18-19 NLT

It's hard to save up money. You might be too young to work, so you need your parents to pay for things until you get a few dollars. Or maybe family expenses are high right now and there's not a lot of extra cash to get things you would really like. Money is not the only way we can be rich.

If you don't have a lot of money, but you have a lot of extra time, you can use your time to bless others. What do you do during your free time? Do you watch movies or play games? What ways could you be showing God's love to other people? You can be rich in God's love and choose to share this any time!

PRAYER REQUESTS

Father, thank you for giving us a lot of love. We want to share that love with those in need. Help us to understand that even if we don't have a lot of money, we are rich because you have blessed us with life and with each other.

Give generously to them and do so without a grudging heart; then because of this the LORD your God will bless you in all your work and in everything you put your hand to.

DEUTERONOMY 15:10 NIV

You sometimes get money for doing jobs around the house, or maybe a relative sends you money in a card for your birthday. What do you do with your money when you get it? Do you save it, or do you like to spend it?

Money is a great thing to have, but the Bible warns us not to love it too much. What usually happens when people get a lot of money is that they become greedy. That means they want more and more and more, and they don't like to share. Money is to be used for good and not evil, and to remember that Jesus will always make sure we have what we need.

Let's talk!

How do you feel when you share with others?

How can you choose to spend your money wisely?

PRAISE REPORT

Share recent answers to prayer.

What are you grateful for today?

Go around the table and have each person describe (and write down) one way that they will share their time or possessions this week.

Dear God, it feels good to give to others, like when we share our food, belongings, or money. It feels even better knowing that when we help others, we are helping you! We want to be cheerful givers. Help us to give generously.

DID YOU KNOW?

Most people know Bill Gates as the co-founder of Microsoft, a very successful computer company. But did you know that he is also the most generous person in the world? He has given away 27 billion dollars in his lifetime, which is approximately 32% of his wealth. His mom obviously taught him how to share when he was a little boy.

The Right Outfit

*You are God's chosen people. You are holy
and dearly loved. So put on tender mercy and
kindness as if they were your clothes. Don't be
proud. Be gentle and patient.*

Colossians 3:12 NIRV

What is your favorite thing to wear? Is it a certain pair
of jeans, sweatpants, or a sports shirt? Maybe you
enjoy dressing up in a costume, or perhaps you just like
wearing your pajamas!

The Bible talks about putting on clothes of kindness,
gentleness, and patience. What would that look like?
Wearing those clothes would mean that we would make
decisions to be kind, gentle, loving people all day long.
When we remember to treat others with kindness and
mercy, we will always feel like we are wearing our best
clothes.

PRAYER REQUESTS

*Father God, help us to remember to dress properly each
day, putting on good things like kindness, patience, mercy,
and gentleness, so we are ready to share your love with
everyone we encounter.*

A gentle answer turns away wrath,
but a harsh word stirs up anger.

PROVERBS 15:1 NIV

Let's talk!

What are some steps you can take to become more gentle?

How can you show gentleness even when you don't feel like it?

We all get grumpy sometimes. We shout, we push, we say unkind things. Usually when this happens we get in trouble. This is because adults want you to grow up into a person that treats people with kindness.

God doesn't want us to be mean either, but his first response to your grumpiness is not anger. He wants to show you love even when you have done wrong. When you feel his love, it helps you to be more kind and fair to others.

PRAISE REPORT

Share recent answers to prayer.

What are you grateful for today?

Make a list of things that you need to be gentle with. Now write next to each thing how you can show gentleness.

Dear God, we admire how gentle you are with us. We want to treat others with the same gentleness. It's true that arguments go much more peacefully when answers are gentle instead of angry. Help us to remember that especially when we are feeling frustrated, hurt, or angry.

DID YOU KNOW?

Gorillas may look fierce but they are really quite gentle. These shy vegetarians can weigh up to 430 pounds, which is quite surprising since their diet consists mostly of fruit, leaves, and seeds. They are a constant reminder that you can't always judge the heart by the outward appearance.

Goodness Defined

You have stored up so many good things.
You have stored them up for those
who have respect for you.
You give those things while everyone watches.
You give them to people who run to
you for safety.

PSALM 31:19 NIRV

This verse says that God is storing up good things. What exactly are those good things? Safety? Peace? A quiet heart when life is crazy? Joy even when your best friend is mad at you? It would seem that his goodness could be all of these and much more.

God has so much goodness that he actually has to store it. If he didn't, we would be overwhelmed by it all at once! The goodness of God is for those of us who know and love him. God rewards us more than we could imagine in our wildest dreams when we choose to follow and obey him.

PRAYER REQUESTS

God, we trust in your goodness. Thank you that you store up so many good things for those who love you. We have been so blessed by you and we acknowledge that today.

Everything God created is good, and nothing is to be rejected if it is received with thanksgiving.

1 TIMOTHY 4:4 NIV

God's goodness is great every day; his love is steady and it always fights for us. We can show God how thankful we are by remembering how good he is and telling others about what he has done for us.

Even when life isn't easy, the list of blessings God has given you is very long. This day is beautiful because God loves you and he is so good to you. Tell others about his kindness and mercy this week.

Let's talk!

What's hard about being good all the time?

What are some of the good things God has given you that you really appreciate?

PRAISE REPORT

Share recent answers to prayer.

What are you grateful for today?

Write down definitions of what you think the word good means. Then write a list of good things God has blessed you with. Thank God for his goodness to you and recognize that he is the very definition of good.

Dear God, sometimes things are frustrating. We get irritated or annoyed with family, our friends don't understand us, and things don't go our way. We know you created us to share your goodness with others. Help us to do that even when it's not easy.

DID YOU KNOW?

If you look up "good things," you will stumble upon many physical things that people call good: space savers, fancy water, burgers and fries, stain removers, doorstops, garden tools, pillows, the list goes on and on. There are companies, charities, and foundations that all try to define what goodness is either by selling good products or naming their brand with the word good. God has his own definition of the word, and what we call good pales in comparison.

Circles of Grace

BREAKFAST TIME

The Lord shows mercy and is kind.
He does not become angry quickly,
and he has great love.

PSALM 103:8 ICB

You know when you have done something wrong, and you think your parents are going to yell at you. You expect them to be angry, but instead they treat you kindly. This is one way of demonstrating grace.

God has that kind of love for us. He is full of mercy and grace, which means that he is kind to us even when we have done something wrong. He doesn't get angry quickly and he makes sure that we know of his great love and grace.

PRAYER REQUESTS

Father, thank you for your grace. Help us do the right thing even though we know you will show us kindness no matter what we do. We want to be pleasing to you each day.

Let the words you speak always be full of grace.
Learn how to make your words what people
want to hear. Then you will know how to answer
everyone.

COLOSSIANS 4:6 NIRV

Let's talk!

Can you think
of a time when
you were
shown grace?

How can you
use grace
when you are
with others?

When you throw a rock into a still
pond, what happens? Lots of circles
of water start to show up and they get
bigger and bigger as they go out. This
is what God's grace is like.

When we are given grace, we feel
God's love and can't wait to share
it with others. Then they share our
excitement and also give thanks to
God. This is how we can spread the
love of God all over the world. Let's
give thanks to God!

PRAISE REPORT

Share recent answers to prayer.

What are
you grateful
for today?

Showing grace to others the way Jesus shows grace to us isn't always easy. As a family, set a goal to show grace this week. It could involve forgiving someone when they do or say something mean, helping someone in need, using kind words when you're angry, or showing gratitude to others. Each day, write down a situation where you showed grace and revisit your notes at the end of the week to see how much grace you've shown as a family!

Dear Jesus, your grace gave us forgiveness and love. It's what allows us stay in relationship with you. Help us to act with more grace during our days so we can live like you.

DID YOU KNOW?

Have you heard the saying "as graceful as a swan"? Swans are thought to be graceful creatures with their long, curved neck and ability to effortlessly glide across the water. Although the look of a swan may be graceful, swans can become aggressive while protecting their nest and eggs.

The Trust Walk

*Guide me in your truth and teach me,
for you are God my Savior, and my hope is in
you all day long.*

PSALM 25:5 NIV

When you don't know what to do, remember that God isn't trying to hide the answer from you. He wants you to go down the right path, and he will share his help when you ask.

Quiet down a little bit and listen to God. He will speak to you as you talk with him each day. You will understand his voice more and more.

PRAYER REQUESTS

Heavenly Father, we need your help. Calm our minds and hearts so we can listen to what you say and know where to go. We need your guidance each day to keep us on the right path.

*Those who are led by the Spirit of God
are children of God.*

ROMANS 8:14 NIRV

Have you ever done a trust walk? One person who is able to see the path ahead has to guide their blindfolded friend around obstacles in order for them to arrive safely to the finish line.

Our walk with God is very similar. God knows what lies ahead. If we listen carefully to his voice, he will lead us in the right direction. God always wants to be trusted. It is up to us to learn to know his voice.

Let's talk!

What do you need God to help guide you in today?

How do you hear from God?

PRAISE REPORT

Share recent answers to prayer.

What are you grateful for today?

Play a game of "Follow the Leader." Designate a leader that the rest of the family must line up behind. Have the leader walk around the house while doing various activities. The other family members must mimic the leader's behavior. If someone fails to mimic, they are out of the game. Keep playing until there is only one person left following the leader.

Dear God, sometimes we want to do everything ourselves. We often think we know what's best for us. Help us to stop thinking that way because you are the one who should guide our steps and our lives.

DID YOU KNOW?

The millions of stars that God created can be used as guides! One of the most popular stars to be used as a guide is Polaris, or more commonly known as the North Star. By finding the Big Dipper and Little Dipper constellations, you can identify the North Star. The North Star keeps its spot in the sky and always points true north, helping guide people in the right direction. Next time you're looking up at the stars, see if you can find the North Star!

Run Free

*Anyone who belongs to Christ has become
a new person. The old life is gone;
a new life has begun!*

2 CORINTHIANS 5:17 NLT

Have you ever seen a very dirty car go through a car wash and come out sparkling clean? When we accept Jesus into our hearts, he forgets all the bad, ugly things we have done, and he makes us shiny and new—like that nice clean car.

We all have bad things we would like to forget, like mean words we've said and people we've hurt. Every day, we can tell Jesus we are sorry for our sin and he washes that yucky dirt away.

PRAYER REQUESTS

Jesus, we are so happy that you can take our sin away. Thank you for forgiving us and washing away our dirt so we can be clean. Help us to come to you as soon as we have sinned and ask for forgiveness, so we don't stay dirty for long.

*No, dear brothers and sisters, I have not
achieved it, but I focus on this one thing:
Forgetting the past and looking forward to what
lies ahead.*

PHILIPPIANS 3:13 NLT

Let's talk!

Why doesn't
God want you
to feel guilt
and shame?

How do you
get rid of
your guilt?

Imagine if you were captured and
sent to jail. It would make you so
happy if someone found a way to
rescue you and get you out of jail.
You would run free and never go near
the jail again.

Jesus rescued us from our sin and
we have a fresh start because he has
forgiven us. When we keep feeling
guilty about our sin, it's like going
back to the jail and putting the chains
back on our hands and feet. God
wants us to feel free and good about his forgiveness,
so stay free!

PRAISE REPORT
Share recent answers to prayer.

*What are
you grateful
for today?*

Do the dishes as a family tonight. Find a way for everyone to get involved with either washing or drying. Talk about how no matter how many times the dishes get dirty, they can always be washed clean. Jesus is faithful to forgive us no matter how many times we mess up.

Dear Jesus, we want your forgiveness so we don't feel guilty. Help us to admit our sins and ask for your grace. After that, you say we should forget the past and focus on the future. We need you to help us do this.

DID YOU KNOW?

People have been using soap for over 2,000 years. Groups like the Celts and Phoenicians were both known to make soap by boiling animal fats and mixing it with ashes from a wood fire. They didn't use it to wash their bodies, but rather to cure animal skins or clean their clothes. It was the Romans who first started using soap to wash their bodies. Their idea stuck! Today over ten billion pounds of soap is produced. One third of that is created and consumed the United States alone.

Joyful Service

BREAKFAST TIME

*Be kind and compassionate to one another,
forgiving each other, just as in
Christ God forgave you.*
EPHESIANS 4:32 NIV

It can be fun to look for creative ways to serve other people. You might decide to pick a flower for your mother or do the dishes without being asked. You might make a card for your dad or help take care of someone when they are sick. Maybe you bring cookies to a neighbor who just had a baby. Or babysit someone's children so they can take a break.

The more you look for ways to serve, the more serving will become a part of who you are. Being a person who helps others is something that is truly valued by God.

PRAYER REQUESTS

Jesus, help us to follow your example of serving by finding ways to bless and encourage others who need a helping hand.

DINNER TIME

*In everything I did, I showed you that by this
kind of hard work we must help the weak,
remembering the words the Lord Jesus himself
said: "It is more blessed to give than to receive."*

ACTS 20:35 NIV

Have you seen a homeless person begging in the streets for food or money? It can be confusing to know what to do because they make you feel uncomfortable. Maybe you feel sorry for them, or you don't quite understand.

There are a lot of people that need help—sometimes in our own country and sometimes in other countries. God says that he loves everyone so much and he wants to rescue people that are poor or unloved. Can you be a part of God's plan to help others?

Let's talk!

What do you like people to help you with?

What is something helpful you could do for someone today?

PRAISE REPORT
Share recent answers to prayer.

What are you grateful for today?

Have everyone write down what they could do this week to help someone out. Pull out some blank paper and crayons or markers to create a card to give to someone special. Be sure to include some kind words or draw a creative picture. Drop it in the mail or hand deliver it this week.

Dear Jesus, it feels good to receive help and gifts, but you say it is better to serve others instead. That is a good reminder. We want to love and help people who have less than we do.

DID YOU KNOW?

Amy Carmichael devoted her life to serving the children of India. While working with women from various villages, she realized that several of them had given their children to the temple. This was a horrible practice where children were given to the gods and became temple slaves. Amy worked hard for the rest of her life to abolish this practice by rescuing temple children and educating parents.

Speaking Truth

*It is better to correct someone openly
than to love him and not show it.
The slap of a friend can be trusted to help you.
But the kisses of an enemy are nothing but lies.*
PROVERBS 27:5-6 ICB

It is always better to tell the truth. It might be easier to lie sometimes, but it never feels good on the inside. Even though it is hard to tell the truth, you feel a lot better when you do. When you are truthful, people can trust you.

The next time you want to tell a lie, remember that it will only make you feel worse. Speaking the truth is the best way. It keeps you and others from getting hurt. God loves truth, and he loves you!

PRAYER REQUESTS

God, help us to be brave enough to always tell the truth. Thank you for forgiving us and loving us even when we make mistakes. We want people to be able to trust us, so help us to tell the truth even when it is difficult.

*"Everything that is hidden will become clear,
and every secret thing will be made known."*
LUKE 8:17 NCV

Let's talk!

**What do you
find it most
difficult to be
honest about?**

**How do you
feel when
someone is
untruthful?**

When we break something, or hurt
someone, it can be tempting to tell a
lie about why we did it, or to blame it
on someone else. We lie because we
don't want to get in trouble. But lying
actually makes us feel worse.

Did you know that it is not even
possible for God to tell a lie? God is
so good and so truthful that when
he makes a promise, it has to come
true. When we tell the truth in every
situation, it shows the world a part
of God's character and creates an
atmosphere of trust.

PRAISE REPORT
Share recent answers to prayer.

*What are
you grateful
for today?*

Most of us remember Aesop's Fable about the boy who cried wolf. The boy lied to the villagers three times telling them that a wolf was coming for their sheep. Eventually a real wolf approached but when the boy cried for help no one came because they thought he was just trying to trick them again. Assign roles to each family member and have fun acting out this story.

Dear Jesus, we want to be like you and follow your laws. We know that honesty is important. Help us to always be truthful to those around us. Thank you for your example of speaking truth in love.

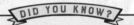

DID YOU KNOW?

People don't call Abraham Lincoln "Honest Abe" for nothing. Once, while working as a store clerk, he accidentally took six cents too much from a customer. After he got off work, he walked three miles to return the six cents to the customer! Abraham went on to be a lawyer and the nickname stuck. His honesty no doubt helped lead him to be elected as the 16th president of the United States.

Hope that Lasts

*Hope will never bring us shame. That's because
God's love has poured into our hearts.
This happened through the Holy Spirit,
who has been given to us.*

ROMANS 5:5 NIRV

When we hope for things and never get them, it can be discouraging. When we do get something we hoped for, we often find the excitement wears off and we transfer our hope to something else. The reality is that anything we hope for in this life (that won't carry into eternity) won't keep us satisfied for very long.

We trust God and put our hope in him because what he promises us is true. When Jesus died on the cross and then rose again, he gave us hope that lasts forever. We know that every promise Jesus makes will come true.

PRAYER REQUESTS

Holy God, we trust that you keep all your promises and we will always have hope because of you. Thank you that your hope lasts forever, and that we will never be disappointed when you give us what you have promised.

The LORD is good to those whose hope is in him,
to the one who seeks him.

LAMENTATIONS 3:25 NIV

Would you put an apple in the toaster, or some honey on your toothbrush? Would you put your shoes in the dishwasher, or your brush in the oven? No! You've got to put things in the right place if you want to be able to find them later or keep them from being ruined.

The Bible says that the right place for hope is in Jesus. Hope is all about believing in the best for your future, and Jesus is the only one who is going to give you the very best future. So hope in Jesus!

Let's talk!

What things have you hoped for in the past?

What things can you hope for that will not disappoint you?

PRAISE REPORT
Share recent answers to prayer.

What are you grateful for today?

Write the word *HOPE* vertically on this page. Then create an acrostic of God's promises by writing down words that start with each letter of the word.

Dear God, thank you for giving us hope that is alive. Jesus died for us and gave us the gift of the Holy Spirit. Help us to seek you in everything we do because we know that you will never let us down.

DID YOU KNOW?

Martin Luther was studying to be a lawyer but changed his course of study after being struck by lightning. He began to study the Bible as a monk and then he put his hope in Jesus for salvation. This was a new idea to Christians in his day who thought they had to achieve their salvation with good deeds and by giving money to the church. "Everything that is done in this world is done by hope." –Martin Luther

Honor Due

This is how we know what real love is:
Jesus gave his life for us. So we should give
our lives for our brothers.

1 JOHN 3:16 ICB

There isn't a better example of love than Jesus Christ. He gave up his entire life for love. He left the beautiful heavens and came down to earth so we could spend forever with him. He did what was best for us!

While many of us won't actually have to die for another person, there are plenty of ways to show our love for others. The best way to show love is to think about what is best for the other person just like Jesus did for us.

PRAYER REQUESTS

Jesus, thank you for giving up your life in heaven and coming to earth to rescue us from sin. Help us to love others the way you love us, by preferring them over ourselves.

*Humble yourselves under the mighty power
of God, and at the right time he will
lift you up in honor.*

1 PETER 5:6 NLT

Let's talk!

How can you
honor someone
today?

Is it difficult for
you to listen
to people in
authority over
you? Why do
you think that is
or isn't?

The older people in our lives are
placed there for a reason. We need
help. Sometimes it's hard to obey
parents, bosses, or teachers. We
might not want to do what they are
asking us to do. We might not like
what they are saying. Often, these
people are trying to do what is best
for us.

One of the ten commandments is
to honor your parents. It's the only
commandment with a promise
attached: honor your parents, and
it will go well with you. Instead of
arguing about how your way is better
or complaining about what you are being asked to do,
honor your parents through obedience. You might be
surprised how your attitude changes.

PRAISE REPORT

Share recent answers to prayer.

What are
you grateful
for today?

There are many ways we can prefer one another in our daily lives. Stepping in and helping someone with their chores or responsibilities is an easy way to show that you love them. Could you offer to clear your brother or sister's dishes tonight? Pick a job that someone else usually does in your family and offer to take care of it this week. Write down what you will do this week to show honor.

Dear God, you honor us and ask us to honor others. We should put them before ourselves in honor. Help us to be humble and kind. We want to be more like you every day.

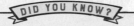

DID YOU KNOW?

Other than Jesus, perhaps the best example we have of people preferring others before themselves is in the lives of missionaries. Charles Thomas Studd was a famous British cricket player, which is kind of like baseball, so picture Joe DiMaggio. Charles knew that fame and fortune would soon go away, so he gave it all up to join the China Inland Mission. He chose to spend his life serving God and loving people. The lasting impact that he had on both China and India proves that he chose wisely by preferring others!

A Humble Heart

God continues to give us more grace.
That's why Scripture says,
"God opposes those who are proud.
But he gives grace to those who are humble."

JAMES 4:6 ESV

If you were playing a game with friends and someone got bossy, telling everyone that they had to play by their rules, how would you feel? Would you want to do it their way? Now think of someone who kindly says that there might be a better way to play the game. You would probably listen.

Jesus wants to listen to people when they ask him with a good heart. If you try to tell him to do it your way, it doesn't show that you care about what is best. Being humble means listening to Jesus. And when you listen to him, he will give you grace.

PRAYER REQUESTS

Jesus, thank you that you created us to need you. Help us to know that you always have the best way in mind. We want to show humility in how we live and in how we ask you for things.

DINNER TIME

Pride will ruin people,
but those who are humble will be honored.

PROVERBS 29:23 NCV

It's okay to want to be noticed for the good things you do, but there are times when we need to think about others before we show off. What does it feel like when someone says that they are the best at throwing a ball, or drawing a picture, or doing math?

God looks at the heart, and he wants us to be good and kind to everyone. Instead of bragging about yourself, tell others about how amazing they are. This is the kind of heart that God thinks is good.

Let's talk!

Can you describe a time when you showed humility instead of pride?

How does it make you feel when people listen to your ideas?

PRAISE REPORT
Share recent answers to prayer.

What are you grateful for today?

God loves it when we pray with a humble heart. A big part of being humble is taking time to listen to God and not just talk to him. Pray as a family for God to give you a humble heart and ears to hear what he wants to tell you. Be sure to include a time of silence as you listen to God. If this is new to you just try it for thirty seconds. Step out in faith and share with each other whatever you think God might have said during this time.

Dear God, we don't want to be prideful, but sometimes we act that way, especially when we feel insecure. We want to be kind and humble toward our friends and family. We want them to see you in us. Help us to have more humility.

DID YOU KNOW?

The Bible calls Moses a very humble man, more humble than any other man on earth! It's no wonder God chose him to be the one to lead the Israelites out of captivity in Egypt.

Good Character

He knows how we were made.
He remembers that we are dust.

PSALM 103:14 ICB

Can you jump higher than a building? Can you walk through walls? Can you walk on water? Of course not! Our bodies weren't made to do things like that. There are plenty of amazing things about how our bodies were created and how they work, but we weren't made to be invincible.

When God made our bodies, he didn't make a mistake. We were created to live a great life, but God didn't want us to be superheroes. He wants us to be the best we can be and leave the rest to him. Being our best is enough!

PRAYER REQUESTS

Father, you designed us exactly how you wanted us each to be. Help us to love the bodies that you have given us and to keep them healthy. Teach us to do our best and to leave the rest to you. Thank you for accepting us just as we are.

The honest person will live in safety,
but the dishonest will be caught.

PROVERBS 10:9 NCV

Let's talk!

What does
integrity mean
to you?

Do you admire
the integrity
of anyone in
your life?

We can all fake good character. We
can play the part of a good Christian:
go to church, read the Bible, and
follow the rules when people are
watching. But what choices do we
make when we're alone? Do we
consistently do what is honorable and
right even when there is no reward,
even when no one is watching? Do
we cheat if we know we won't get
caught? Do we cut corners instead of
doing our very best?

Integrity, not hypocrisy, is what God wants for us. The
Lord sees through all our attempts to be something we
aren't, so pretending with him is a waste of time. He
would rather we be upfront and honest. Not only will
our relationship with him improve but the rewards with
others will come too. People will learn to trust our words
and depend on our character.

PRAISE REPORT
Share recent answers to prayer.

What are
you grateful
for today?

Have everyone write down two things they are really good at, and one thing that they are not so good at. Go around the table and have everyone read their lists out loud. Remind each other that God doesn't expect us to be perfect, but he does want us to do the best we can with what we have.

Dear God, living with integrity means being honest and pure at all times. We know we are not perfect, but we know how you want us to live. Help us to be good examples of integrity to those around us. Help us to act the same whether we think people are watching us or not.

DID YOU KNOW?

Michael Phelps starting swimming when he was seven because his mom wanted him to learn. It turns out, he fell in love with the sport. By the age of ten, Phelps held the national record for 100-meter butterfly. He competed in his first Olympic games in Sydney 2000. In 2004, he won six gold medals in Athens. At the Beijing Olympics in 2008, he won an all-time record eight gold medals. With six medals in 2012 and another six in 2016, his total medal count is 28. This made him the most decorated athlete in Olympic history!

Fullest Joy

BREAKFAST TIME

"I loved you as the Father loved me. Now remain in my love I have obeyed my Father's commands, and I remain in his love. In the same way, if you obey my commands, you will remain in my love. I have told you these things so that you can have the same joy I have. I want your joy to be the fullest joy."

JOHN 15:9-11 ICB

Joy comes into our lives when we follow God's directions. He rewards us with a whole lot of love. As we stay in this love, we become full of joy that can be shared with the people around us.

Can you think of anyone that needs more joy in their life? Most people have busy schedules these days and it seems that this busyness causes a lot of stress. Maybe you can help people who seem tense by being a happy person yourself. Happy people are pleasant to be around, and this is a good representation of Jesus.

PRAYER REQUESTS

Thank you, God, for your love that gives us so much joy. Help us to share our joy with those around us. Help us to be happy people that others enjoy being with.

May the God of hope fill you with all joy and peace as you trust in him, so that you may overflow with hope by the power of the Holy Spirit.

ROMANS 15:13 NIV

Some days are harder than others. The sun doesn't shine or the day just feels impossible. Thankfully, God has given us joy that doesn't depend on what's going on around us.

God's joy brings us out of hiding and shows us the beautiful things around us in the middle of a sometimes dark and stormy world. God has given us his joy as a gift. We can choose to be joyful each day. Will you choose joy this week?

Let's talk!

What things make you happy?

How does God make you joyful?

PRAISE REPORT

Share recent answers to prayer.

What are you grateful for today?

Write down the names of everyone at the table. Next to their name, write down how they bring joy to the family. Remember to encourage these qualities in each other.

Dear God, thank you for joy. Thank you for letting us laugh with our friends and joke with our family. We are so happy that we belong to you. You fill us with delight even when life is hard. We are so grateful for your gift of joy.

DID YOU KNOW?

Smiles are contagious they say, and it's true! We naturally smile when smiled at. We even have a hard time creating a frown in response to someone who is smiling at us. It's not just our facial muscles that are affected, smiling instantly lifts our mood. God created our bodies to release endorphins that make us happy when we smile or laugh. Maybe laughter really is the best medicine.

Showing Kindness

*"Is there anyone still left in Saul's family?
I want to show kindness to this person
for Jonathan's sake!"*

2 SAMUEL 9:1 ICB

When you meet your friend's brother or sister, father or mother, you know that you should be polite and nice because you want to do the right thing for your friend.

King David did this in the Bible. He loved his friend Jonathan so much that he asked if there was anyone else that he could be kind to because he wanted to honor his friend. What would happen if we asked that question each day? Is there anyone we can show kindness to today?

PRAYER REQUESTS

God, remind us to ask who we can show kindness to each day. Help us to listen to your voice and to be great friends to others. There are so many ways we can bless those around us. Give us ideas for how we can best show kindness to others.

*Kind people do themselves a favor,
but cruel people bring trouble on themselves.*
PROVERBS 11:17 NCV

Let's talk!

What wrong things have been fixed in your life?

What is something kind you can do for someone today?

Have you ever been blamed for something you didn't do? It doesn't seem fair. When life is unfair, it is hard to remember that God knows all things. He also knows the wrong things we have done and he forgives us for them.

Take a minute to think about how God has already fixed some of the wrong things in your life. Is there a person in your life that you can show kindness to—the way God shows kindness to you?

PRAISE REPORT

Share recent answers to prayer.

What are you grateful for today?

Write the letters K-I-N-D-N-E-S-S on this page vertically. Now come up with a way to show kindness beginning with each letter.

Dear Jesus, your kindness is supposed to be an example for us to live by. It's not always easy to be kind, but that's how we can show your love to others. Help us to be more kind with our friends, family, and those who cross our paths each day.

DID YOU KNOW?

Perhaps no human being embodied kindness more than Mother Teresa. She spent her life caring for the sick and the homeless: the people that society wished to forget. Even after her own death, Mother Teresa's kindness still has a global impact through the organization she started named The Sisters of the Missionaries of Charity. This charity continues to care for people in 123 countries around the world.

Fearless Leader

In all these things we are more than conquerors through him who loved us.

ROMANS 8:37 NIV

Imagine you are fighting a battle with all your might. There are swords flying and warriors falling. Your eyes are drawn toward your fearless leader slaying dragons right and left. Enemies who dare attack him lose terribly because he has so much power and he is incredibly skilled. That leader is Jesus, and he fights for you!

Jesus fills us with his strength to face everything that comes our way. He is on our side, and nothing can keep us down. Nothing can defeat us. Nothing we are going through is too hard for Jesus to help give us victory over. All we have to do is keep our eyes fixed on him and ask him for help.

PRAYER REQUESTS

Jesus, thank you for fighting our battles with us and for us. We want to get into the habit of turning to you each time we need help. We know that you hear us and you see us. Through you, we can be more than conquerors!

Without wise leadership, a nation falls;
there is safety in having many advisers.
PROVERBS 11:14 NLT

Have you ever been lost in a store and couldn't find your parents? It can be pretty scary. All it takes is to walk in a different direction or hide behind a bench and suddenly you don't know where your family has gone!

We have to follow Jesus closely. He always knows where we are, but we need to make sure we know where he is and where he wants us to go. Follow him by remembering to love him in everything that you do.

Let's talk!

In what ways can you be a good leader?

How can you be a good follower?

PRAISE REPORT
Share recent answers to prayer.

What are you grateful for today?

Play a few games of thumb wrestling in pairs. Although thumb wrestling isn't a serious battle, it sure is fun to win. Is there someone who seems to win more than others? How would it feel to win every time you played? With Jesus on your side, you can win every battle you face.

Dear Jesus, you are our true leader, and we want to learn from you. It is good to have leaders in our lives so we can learn to be leaders too. Help us to set a good example for others by showing them honesty and love.

DID YOU KNOW?

The peace sign that we commonly make with our fingers (index and middle finger raised like we're saying "2"), was actually a sign that Winston Churchill made popular during WWII. It didn't stand for peace, it actually symbolized victory. Churchill's "V for Victory" sign was used frequently by the Allies during the war to show solidarity with each other and defiance against the enemy.

Love of Learning

*"The seed on good soil stands for those with
an honest and good heart. Those people hear
the message. They keep it in their hearts. They
remain faithful and produce a good crop."*

LUKE 8:15 NIRV

When you plant a seed, you push it deeply into the soil.
A seed won't grow if it is put on a rock because there is
nothing for it to dig its roots into.

Sometimes we hear things from God, but we don't really
listen. This is like being a seed that gets put on a rock.
What we hear can be forgotten and we don't let our
life change. When we hear God's words, we need to
remember them. Write them down, memorize them. That
way, we will be able to understand more about God.

PRAYER REQUESTS

*Lord, thank you that you speak to us. Thank you for
your words of truth that we find in the Bible. Help us to
remember your words so we can understand more about you.*

Those who get wisdom do themselves a favor,
and those who love learning will succeed.

PROVERBS 19:8 NCV

Let's talk!

What helps you learn?

What do you like learning about most?

You might not like having to go to school or doing school work at home. But do you know that getting an education is actually a privilege? There are many children around the world who don't get the opportunity to learn how to read and write.

We learn some pretty important things at school that help us when we grow up. The Bible tells us to listen carefully to wisdom. Whether your teacher is at public school, private school, or home, they have a lot of wisdom to share with you. So listen carefully, and don't waste the opportunity to learn new things.

PRAISE REPORT
Share recent answers to prayer.

What are you grateful for today?

Write this week's verse on a piece of paper and tape it to your bathroom mirror. Make a point to read it out loud several times this week. Before you know it, God's truth will be planted deep in your heart.

Dear God, learning isn't always fun, but we know it is something we need to do. Help us to enjoy the learning that comes from you because it will teach us how you want us to live.

DID YOU KNOW?

Bats—the only flying mammal—navigate and hunt their prey by emitting high-frequency sounds and using their funnel-shaped ears to listen for the echoes those sounds make as they bounce off nearby objects. By using this echolocation, they can pinpoint tiny insects in complete darkness. As bats fly through the air, they emit sounds. Based on the frequency and intensity of the returning echoes, they can tell how far away objects are.

Always Near

The LORD is faithful;
he will strengthen you and
guard you from the evil one.

2 THESSALONIANS 3:3 NLT

Faithful friends stand up for you. A faithful dog sticks close to your side. God is more faithful than either of these! He will never leave you. Even if you feel like you are in the middle of a battle, he will be right there fighting with you.

If people are saying unkind or untrue things about you, God will remind you of what he loves about you. If you feel like nobody cares, God will remind you that he does. He will always help you find joy and peace in your life if you take the time to ask him.

PRAYER REQUESTS

God, we feel much stronger knowing that you are near. Help us to sense your peace and joy when we feel like we are in the middle of a battle and also when things are going well. You are with us all the time and we are so thankful to you for that.

DINNER TIME

The Lord is near to all who call on him,
yes, to all who call on him in truth.

Psalm 145:18 NLT

Isn't this verse wonderful? God says in his Word that he will never leave us. No matter where we go, we cannot be alone. When we are afraid, he is with us. When we don't know what to do, he is with us. When we are sad, he is with us. And in our happy moments, he is there too!

Let's talk!

When do you feel lonely?

How do you feel knowing that God is always with you?

There is no getting away from God, so don't even try. Delight in his nearness and thank him for staying close by your side. Ask him for help whenever you need it and share your special moments with him too. He loves to hear from you.

PRAISE REPORT
Share recent answers to prayer.

What are you grateful for today?

Have each family member draw a picture of themselves in the middle of a battle, be sure to include God fighting with you. When you're done, take turns explaining what you drew.

Dear God, sometimes we feel lonely, but it's nice to know we are never truly alone even if other people are not around. You are always near us and you listen to us when we call out to you.

DID YOU KNOW?

Beavers are known for their hard work but they are also very faithful partners? These loyal, flat-tailed friends mate for life, which is on average about ten years. It's no wonder they have to work so hard since they can have up to four babies at a time, who are called kits. Thankfully they share responsibilities when it comes to raising kits, which momma beavers must greatly appreciate.

Choosing Love

Love is patient and kind. Love is not jealous, it does not brag, and it is not proud. Love is not rude, is not selfish, and does not become angry easily. Love does not remember wrongs done against it. Love takes no pleasure in evil, but rejoices over the truth. Love patiently accepts all things. It always trusts, always hopes, and always continues strong.

1 CORINTHIANS 13:4-7 ICB

You are patient and kind. You are not jealous, you do not brag, you are not rude or selfish. You don't become angry easily, and you don't remember when people do wrong things to you. Does that sound like you? Does it sound like anyone you know?

Love is not just something you feel, but something you choose, even when you don't want to. It means putting other's needs before your own just like Jesus did.

PRAYER REQUESTS

Jesus, you have shown us so much love and patience. When we read these verses, it seems like it is impossible to love the way you do! Teach us how to love and help us to put others first.

Three things will last forever—faith, hope, and love—and the greatest of these is love.

1 CORINTHIANS 13:13 NLT

Let's talk!

What is your definition of love?

How can you share some of God's love with others?

Love comes in a lot of different shapes and sizes. Moms and dads love each other in a different way than they love their children. Siblings love each other, but not quite the same as they love their friends. We love food, we love sports, we love art… so what is love really?

The Bible tells us that God is love. It says that love, like God, is patient, kind, and enduring. Love, like God, never fails. The only true definition for love is God himself. We will never be able to find anyone who loves us as well as God does, but we can learn from his example and try to love others like he loves us.

PRAISE REPORT

Share recent answers to prayer.

What are you grateful for today?

Brainstorm as many ideas you can about how you can show love to others. Write them down and then circle your favorite three. Aim to complete those three acts of love this week.

Dear Jesus, you teach us that love is an important characteristic. You don't just love when it's easy. You love all the time. We want to use your love as an example of how to love others.

DID YOU KNOW?

Forrest Lunsway certainly knew about patient love! At the age of 72, he began to pursue a widow named Rose Pollard. She liked spending time with Forrest but kept telling him she had no interest in being his wife. Their friendship continued but Forrest never gave up on the idea of marrying Rose. After 20 years of pursuing her, he proposed! Rose said no, but joked that if he lived to be 100, she would then marry him. So, eight years later, on his 100th birthday, Forrest and Rose were married at last!

The Best Way

*Restore to me the joy of your salvation,
and make me willing to obey you.*
PSALM 51:12 NLT

Do you remember a time when you didn't want to do what your parents asked you to do? Maybe they told you to go upstairs and brush your teeth and you chose to ignore them because you didn't want to go to bed. Maybe a teacher or a boss asked you to complete a task you didn't really want to do, so you pretended to forget about it. We have a lot of choices to obey every single day whether we are young or old.

You probably know that in the end it feels really good to do the right thing! Your choices affect other people. When you obey, it makes people happy, and it usually makes you feel happy too. God loves it when we are joyful about obeying him.

PRAYER REQUESTS

God, your way is the best way. Help us to choose to obey you and to be joyful about obeying others you have put in our lives as leaders. We trust you with our lives.

DINNER TIME

Children, obey your parents in everything,
for this pleases the Lord.
COLOSSIANS 3:20 NIV

Sometimes it can be annoying listening to and obeying those in authority over us. It can seem like they are just trying to boss us around. Often their motivations are good though, and we should try to believe that before assuming the worst.

God gives us directions and tells us the best way to live. Sometimes it seems that following God is like following a bunch of rules. But God has given us rules so we can live our lives safely and happily. He really does want the best for us.

Let's talk!

Why is it important to be obedient?

How can you be obedient this week?

PRAISE REPORT
Share recent answers to prayer.

What are you grateful for today?

Play a few rounds of "Mother May I?" Everyone line up at one end of the room with the designated Mother standing at the opposite end with her back to the group. Each person in the group takes a turn asking, "Mother may I take (insert #) steps forward." The Mother can choose to grant or deny each request. The first person to reach the Mother takes his or her place and then the group returns to their starting positions and a new round begins.

Dear God, sometimes we know what we should do, but we don't do it. And sometimes we know what we shouldn't do and we do it anyway. That is disobedience, and we don't want to act that way. Help us to obey those in authority over us and most of all, help us to be obedient to you.

DID YOU KNOW?

Little puppies might not seem very obedient, always wanting to play and jump on you. But with positive training they can learn to obey quickly! Most dogs can learn more than 1000 words. Some common tricks dogs learn are to sit, shake, lie down, dance, roll over, and play dead.

Waiting Patiently

Let's not get tired of doing what is good.
At just the right time we will reap a harvest
of blessing if we don't give up.

GALATIANS 6:9 NLT

When you plant a seed in a pot and wait for it to grow,
it can take a very long time for a little sprout to show.
Wouldn't it take even longer to see flowers on the plant?

God says that sometimes the results of our good works
can take time to start showing, just like that seed being
planted in a pot. We need to have patience and keep
doing good. At the right time, God will show us the good
that has come from doing the right thing.

PRAYER REQUESTS

Father, we want to follow your perfect example of patience.
Help us to be patient while we wait for the results of our
good works to show.

Be completely humble and gentle; be patient,
bearing with one another in love.

EPHESIANS 4:2 NIV

Let's talk!

What things do
you tend to get
most impatient
about?

What helps
you to be
patient when
you get
frustrated?

Have you ever gone to an amusement
park and had to wait in line for a
really long time to get on a ride?
Maybe you have been to a movie and
had to wait a while before it started. It
can be hard to wait!

God has promised that one day he
will make everything right on earth
again. We will have a new heaven
and a new earth and there will be no
more trouble. But we have to wait!
Can you wait patiently? The Bible
says to be patient and to keep on
praying, because it will happen!

PRAISE REPORT

Share recent answers to prayer.

**What are
you grateful
for today?**

Make a list of things that test your patience. Now write down a possible solution for each that will enable you to keep your cool when these things happen.

Dear God, patience is hard to practice, but you value patience over anger. We want to please you and treat others with love. When we feel like getting angry with someone, help us to think of you and be patient instead.

DID YOU KNOW?

Today it takes builders only a few months to construct an average home. It took the Egyptians over twenty years to build the Pyramid in Giza! This colossal structure contains over two million stones. It's believed to have had over 100,000 people working together to get the huge pyramid built, and it still stands today. Those people had to wait a very long time to see their work completed.

Gift of Peace

BREAKFAST TIME

*"I am leaving you with a gift—peace of mind
and heart. And the peace I give is a gift the
world cannot give. So don't be troubled
or afraid."*

JOHN 14:27 NLT

Everybody likes to get presents! Can you think of a time
when you got a gift that you really, really wanted? Or
something that you had never be given before?

Jesus describes peace as a gift like this. It's something
that only he can give. It's not something that anyone
in this world could wrap up for you. It's one of the best
gifts because peace helps us to be calm when things are
tough. Open up his gift of peace today.

PRAYER REQUESTS

*Jesus, thank you for giving us the gift of peace. When
things seem crazy, or chaotic, or stressful, help us to
remember that we don't have to be nervous or unsettled
because you are with us.*

DINNER TIME

May the Lord of peace himself give you
peace at all times and in every way.
The Lord be with all of you.

2 THESSALONIANS 3:16 NIV

Have you ever seen a baby sleeping? Have you been outside and realized that everything was quiet? What about a time when you were quietly drawing and nobody was around to mess things up? These are moments of peace.

God loves peace! He loves it so much that he gives you peace. Sometimes life is too busy or too noisy or too scary. In those times, ask God for his peace in your heart and thank him for being the only source of true peace.

Let's talk!

When do you need to remember the peace God gives you?

What images do you see when you think of peace?

PRAISE REPORT
Share recent answers to prayer.

What are you grateful for today?

Write a list of things that make you feel peaceful. Spend some time quietly reflecting on these things now.

Dear God, we need to remember that you have given us the gift of peace. Our lives won't always be easy, but you say we never need to be unsettled or afraid. Thank you for winning our battles for us.

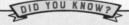

DID YOU KNOW?

The United States received a pretty big gift from France over 100 years ago. The Statue of Liberty was built in France and then all 350 individual pieces were shipped across the ocean to be put back together again. She stands 305 feet tall on Liberty Island in New York. If you visited the Statue of Liberty today, you would have to climb 354 steps to reach her crown!

Deserved Praise

Your love is better than life. I will praise you.
I will praise you as long as I live.
I will lift up my hands in prayer to your name.
I will be content as if I had eaten the best foods.
My lips will sing. My mouth will praise you.
PSALM 63:3-5 ICB

What could be better than spending a day at a fun park, eating your favorite food, and laughing with your friends or family? The writer of Psalms thought that Jesus' love was better than anything he had ever experienced in his life.

Do you think you could agree with the psalmist? God is so good to us, and he has blessed us with many amazing things to show us his love. Let's take some time today to praise him for the wonderful life he has given us.

PRAYER REQUESTS

God, your love is better than anything in this life! Help us to remember your many blessings as we go about the day. We want to praise you for your continued faithfulness and goodness to us.

Praise the LORD from the skies.
Praise him high above the earth.
Praise him, sun and moon.
Praise him, all you shining stars.
Let them praise the LORD, because they
were created by his command.

PSALM 148:1,3,5 NCV

Some people say it's the little things that matter, but they aren't always talking about things that are small in size. There are things that happen every day without us even thinking about them. These things might seem small, but they are actually very important. Like hearts beating or bees making honey.

Let's talk!

How do you praise God?

What things can you praise God for today?

Sometimes children notice things that grown-ups don't really pay attention to anymore. They stop to smell the flowers and watch the ants collect food. They praise God for the sun and the moon and the trees. We are all precious to God, and he loves it when we thank him for the wonderful things he has created.

PRAISE REPORT

Share recent answers to prayer.

What are you grateful for today?

Write a song of praise to God from your family. Have each person help create a line or two that gives glory to God for all he is and all he has done. God delights in our praises. He loves when we take time to create special songs to him from our hearts.

Dear God, you deserve so much more praise than we can give. Even the sun and moon cannot give you enough praise. Thank you for all the blessings you have given us and thank you for sending your Son to save us.

DID YOU KNOW?

A male songbird can sing about 2,000 songs in one day. If a songbird never slept, he would sing a different song every forty-five seconds. Can you imagine singing that many songs?

Ongoing Conversation

Don't worry about anything; instead, pray about everything. Tell God what you need, and thank him for all he has done. Then you will experience God's peace, which exceeds anything we can understand. His peace will guard your hearts and minds as you live in Christ Jesus.

PHILIPPIANS 4:6-7 NLT

The great thing about God is that he always knows what you need. When you need someone to talk to, he's there. When you need help, he's there. He is never going to leave you, and he is always delighted to hear from you.

We can pray to God even when we don't feel like we need anything. God wants to hear from us whether we're experiencing something good, bad, or something in between. When we talk to him, he gives our hearts peace because we know that he listens carefully, and he is big enough to take care of us.

PRAYER REQUESTS

Lord, we give you our highs and lows today. Thank you for the joy that you have brought to us, and for your peace in the middle of trouble. We are so grateful that you listen to us when we talk. Help us to be better listeners too.

The LORD does not listen to the wicked,
but he hears the prayers of those who do right.

PROVERBS 15:29 NCV

Do you ever wonder what to pray about? It can be hard to think of things. The Bible says that you can start by praying for people. You could ask God to bring happiness to children in other countries, or to help kids at school to be brave. You can pray for everyone you know, like your teachers, people at church, and your own family. We should even pray for our country's leaders so they can lead us better.

Let's talk!

Do you find it difficult to find things to pray about?

What can you pray about right now?

If you think of people, you will have a lot to pray for. God loves it when you spend time with him praying for others and sharing what is on your heart. He is always ready to listen to what you have to say.

PRAISE REPORT
Share recent answers to prayer.

What are you grateful for today?

Let's play the High and Low game! Going around the table, have everyone share one high and low point of their day. Take a moment to pray at the end, being sure to thank God for being with you in both the highs and lows of your day.

Dear God, sometimes we don't talk to you as much as we should. You want to hear from us when good and bad things happen in our lives. Help us to never stop communicating with you. Thank you for hearing us whenever we speak.

We pray because we have a God who listens and wants to be a part of our lives. Prayer is also good for our health! Multiple scientific studies have shown that people who pray regularly are healthier and live longer lives. Perhaps its greatest medicinal benefit is that prayer reduces stress, and too much stress can make us sick. No wonder God wants us to pray. When we do, we strengthen both our spirit and our body.

Cage of Protection

When I am afraid,
I will put my confidence in you.
Yes, I will trust the promises of God.
And since I am trusting him,
what can mere man do to me?

PSALM 56:3-4 TLB

Have you ever seen a bird in a cage with a cat sitting outside watching the bird? If you haven't seen it in real life, you many have seen it in a number of cartoons or shows. If there were no cage, the bird would be really afraid, but the bird knows that it is safe inside its cage.

We can feel as strong and sure as that little bird in the cage because we have the best protection of all—our Heavenly Father. That cat might be sitting outside the cage waiting to pounce, but we can trust that God is faithful, and he is taking good care of us.

PRAYER REQUESTS

God, when we are afraid, help us to know that you can erase all our fears. When we feel like bad things are trying to get to us, help us feel safe and secure in your cage of protection, knowing you care for us and you are watching over us.

The LORD is good, a refuge in times of trouble.
He cares for those who trust in him.
NAHUM 1:7 NIV

Let's talk!

What do you feel like you need protection from?

How does it make you feel to know God is always there to protect you?

When you have a bad dream, what do you do? When you are afraid, who do you talk to? Did you know that King David in the Bible had a lot of scary moments? Sometimes he even feared for his life! Whenever David was afraid, he went to God for protection and safety. You can do the same thing!

When you are a child of God, you can count on him to keep you safe. This doesn't mean that you will never feel afraid, or that you won't ever hurt yourself. It means that you can trust that God knows what is best for you and that he is watching out for you. He will pick you up when you fall, and he will cover you with his blanket of safety when you run to him.

PRAISE REPORT
Share recent answers to prayer.

What are you grateful for today?

Put a toy under an upside-down drinking glass on the table. Take a small rubber ball and roll it toward the toy. Do you think the toy needs to be worried about the ball hitting it when the toy is under the glass? Now take the glass away and roll the ball toward the toy. Is it possible to knock the toy over when it's not protected by the glass? How is this like the lesson we read earlier?

Dear God, we feel safe knowing you are always watching over us. We never have to fear the evil things of this world. Thank you for being our protector and defender. Help us to think of you the next time we are afraid.

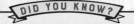

DID YOU KNOW?

Orangutan mothers are very protective of their young. They never put their babies down and often nurse them through the first six or seven years of life. They spend a large amount of time high up in the trees building new nests every day. It would be pretty difficult for a predator to get to that baby orangutan when it's holding onto its mother.

For a Purpose

We know that in all things God works for the good of those who love him, who have been called according to his purpose.

ROMANS 8:28 NIV

What do you dream of doing one day? Can you think of a job that you want to have? Maybe you have a list of exciting places you want to visit, or people you would like to meet.

God has a purpose for your life. He wants you to do things you love, and he wants you to do those while you are loving and following him. You might not know what your purpose in life is, but you will find it when you choose to love God with all of your heart.

PRAYER REQUESTS

God, thank you that you have created us each with things we really enjoy. Help us to find our purpose, as individuals and as a family, in loving and serving you.

My child, pay attention to my words;
listen closely to what I say.
Don't ever forget my words;
keep them always in mind.

PROVERBS 4:20-21 NCV

When you are too tired to get dressed, or put on your shoes, or when you don't know what to make for lunch, you have parents who will help you. You can't drive yourself to school, but your parents will. You can't take yourself to the doctor, but your parents will. Your parents help you a lot in life.

God also helps you. He gave you parents and other kind adults to look after you. He has a good future for you, and even when you can't or don't know how to do great things in life, God will do them with you.

Let's talk!

What do you want to be doing in five years?

Can you think of what God might want you to do with your life?

PRAISE REPORT
Share recent answers to prayer.

What are you grateful for today?

Have everyone write down two things they would like to do some day. Choose one person to read the wish list out loud. After each wish is read, see if everyone can guess who wrote it down.

Dear God, thank you that you have a great purpose for each of our lives. Help us to walk closely with you, so we don't get distracted by other things. You want what is best for us and we trust you to show us what that is.

DID YOU KNOW?

Among the top job choices for kids are a dancer, an actor, a musician, a teacher, a scientist, an athlete, a firefighter, a detective, a writer, a police officer, an astronaut, a pilot, a veterinarian, a lawyer, and a doctor. But the most popular overall dream job selected by kids recently was a video game designer.

Showing Respect

First, I tell you to pray for all people. Ask God for the things people need, and be thankful to him. You should pray for kings and for all who have authority. Pray for the leaders so that we can have quiet and peaceful lives—lives full of worship and respect for God.

1 TIMOTHY 2:1-2 NLT

Who is older than you? Your parents, your teachers, your babysitter, your boss. When you are young, it seems like most people are older than you are. Think about how much older some people are. Is it ten years? Twenty years? Thirty years, or even more?

Older people know more because they have lived a lot longer. If you trust the older people around you, make sure you listen to what they say. Try to understand that they know better than you do. This is what respect is all about.

PRAYER REQUESTS

Father, thank you for the older people in our lives who care about us. Help us to always respect them, and to pay attention when they speak to us. We want to show them that they are valued and important.

Show respect for all people:
Love the brothers and sisters of God's family,
respect God, honor the king.

1 PETER 2:17 NCV

Let's talk!

How can you show respect today?

Who do you think you are supposed to show respect to?

Blessings from God are gifts that he gives us because he loves us. When we respect him, and choose to accept his love, we will want to obey him from our hearts.

The Lord wants to bless us so that we can bless others. We should try to walk closely with God so that we don't miss the chance to bless those close to us.

PRAISE REPORT

Share recent answers to prayer.

What are you grateful for today?

One way we can show respect to others is by showing gratitude. Make a thank you card for a grandparent, a teacher, or someone else who is older than you are. Write a few words to let them know how much you appreciate their impact on your life.

Dear God, sometimes we act rude or disrespectful when we disagree or don't get our own way. You say to show respect for all people and to especially respect and obey our leaders, like parents, teachers, and bosses. Help us to be more respectful to everyone in our lives.

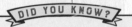

DID YOU KNOW?

Some countries have gone to great lengths to ensure the respect of their elders. China went ahead and made it a law! Parents can actually sue their children if they are neglected emotionally or financially. Koreans have a special party when their parents turn sixty. It's a joyful time for everyone as they celebrate the official beginning of "old age."

Eternal Rewards

Since you became alive again, so to speak, when Christ arose from the dead, now set your sights on the rich treasures and joys of heaven where he sits beside God in the place of honor and power. Let heaven fill your thoughts; don't spend your time worrying about things down here.

COLOSSIANS 3:1-2 TLB

Everyone around us seems to care about clothes and movies and things. Did we get the latest phone, computer, game console, car, or tv? It is hard not to think about material possessions a lot.

The best treasures are in heaven. That's what God wants us to think about more than things on earth. Let's be careful what we watch, look at, and think about. We would do much better to keep our minds on God and his Word.

PRAYER REQUESTS

Father, please help us turn away from the things of this world and set our hearts on heaven. We want to reap eternal rewards that come from obeying and serving you while we are here on earth.

Remember that the Lord will give you an inheritance as your reward, and that the Master you are serving is Christ.

COLOSSIANS 3:24 NLT

Hiking is a really long walk through nature. When you go for a hike, you are usually walking up and down hills or mountains. You can get tired and sore and sometimes slip a few times or have to walk through mud.

You might have heard of a word called *perseverance*. That would be what it takes to walk up a mountain. You have to work hard to get to the top, but it is beautiful when you get there. God will reward you for a life that you live for him.

Let's talk!

Why is the attitude of serving without expecting something back important to God?

What do you need to persevere in this week?

PRAISE REPORT

Share recent answers to prayer.

What are you grateful for today?

It's easy in our society to get overwhelmed with stuff! Most of us probably have a hard time keeping our room clean because we have too many toys. Go through your things this week and set aside one or two items to be dropped off at a donation center. Being selfless and thinking about others is one way we can store up treasures in heaven.

Dear God, it is better to do good deeds without expecting anything in return. Help us to have that kind of attitude when helping others. We look forward to the reward you have for us in heaven.

DID YOU KNOW?

After its inception in 1955, the Guinness Book of World Records quickly went on to become a household name. There are so many people eager for recognition, in 2006 over 100,000 people participated in ten different countries in an attempt to break world records and get their name in the book of fame.

Greater Strength

BREAKFAST TIME

No king is saved by his great army.
No warrior escapes by his great strength.
Horses can't bring victory.
They can't save by their strength.
But the Lord looks after those who fear him.
He watches over those who put their
hope in his love.

PSALM 33:16-18 ICB

Not everyone who can sing well will become famous. The fastest runner at your school might not make it to the Olympics. Sometimes we think that to be the best means that the whole world will notice us. But God didn't give us gifts so that we could be famous; he gave us gifts so that we can show the world his love.

God wants you to do your best with the skills that he has given you, but most of all, he wants you to do it with a good heart.

PRAYER REQUESTS

God, thank you for the gifts you have given us. Help us to do our best with these gifts. We trust that you will show us how to use them for others' good and your glory.

Don't be afraid, for I am with you.
Don't be discouraged, for I am your God.
I will strengthen you and help you.
I will hold you up with my victorious right hand.

ISAIAH 41:10 NLT

Let's talk!

What do you need strength for right now?

How does Jesus make you feel stronger?

Do you know how much power and strength you have? It doesn't feel like it when you are young and smaller than others, but the power comes from Jesus, not from you. It's called the Holy Spirit and he's ready to give you his strength when you don't have any of your own.

God is mighty, and he gladly shares his strength with us so we can face anything like a strong Olympic athlete or a hero!

PRAISE REPORT

Share recent answers to prayer.

What are you grateful for today?

Write down something that the person sitting on your left is really good at. Take a moment as a family to acknowledge each of the strengths that were written down.

Dear God, sometimes we feel as though we have to act tough and strong even when we don't feel that way. It is nice to know it's okay to be weak around you because you give us strength. Thank you for taking care of us.

DID YOU KNOW?

A dung beetle is the strongest insect in the world! They can pull over 1,000 times their body weight, which would be like one of us pulling six double-decker buses full of passengers! When insects play tug-of-war, you can bet the dung beetle gets chosen to be on a team first.

Resisting Temptation

Be sure that no one pays back wrong for wrong.
But always try to do what is good for each other
and for all people.

1 Thessalonians 5:15 ICB

When someone shoves you, do you shove back? If they say something mean, are you mean too? No matter who starts a fight, everyone who is involved will reap some kind of consequence.

It's hard not to fight back, but that's just what God wants us to do. He doesn't want the problem to get worse, so he asks us to do good for each other—even for people who are not very nice. We will always feel better when we choose to do the right thing.

PRAYER REQUESTS

Father God, fill us with your goodness. Help us not to fight back when people upset us. We want to show patience and forgiveness toward others. Help us to bring your peace to troubled situations.

*"Watch and pray so that you will not
fall into temptation. The spirit is willing,
but the flesh is weak."*
MATTHEW 26:41 NIV

Jesus knows what it's like to want
to take the easy way out. When he
knew his death was near, he prayed
for another way. In the end, he made
the choice to do what was the best for
others.

We are supposed to be like Jesus.
Sometimes it is difficult to make the
right decision. It seems like it would be
so much quicker to take the easy path.
We can find strength in Jesus because
he knows how we feel and he will help
us do the right thing.

Let's talk!

What
temptations
do you face
regularly?

What helps
you resist
temptation?

PRAISE REPORT
Share recent answers to prayer.

*What are
you grateful
for today?*

It can be hard to do the right thing in the heat of the moment. Tonight, let's practice ways to respond to difficult situations. Role play scenarios when someone says or does something mean. Write down suggestions for both the right and wrong ways to respond.

Dear God, temptations are hard to deal with for everyone, but you say you always give us a way out of the wrong choices. Please help us to know what the right thing to do is, and then help us to choose it!

DID YOU KNOW?

World War I was a devastating battle that would eventually take the lives of fifteen million soldiers. But on Christmas Day in 1914, both English and German carols could be heard ringing out from the trenches. A truce, or temporary peace, was embraced by approximately two-thirds of the soldiers. Both sides cautiously emerged from their trenches to exchange gifts and participate in makeshift soccer games. What a beautiful example of how the birth of Christ continues to bring peace to the world.

Gratitude First

*Rejoice always, pray continually, give thanks
in all circumstances; for this is God's will for
you in Christ Jesus.*

1 THESSALONIANS 5:16–18 NIV

Sometimes as soon as you wake up in the morning you feel busy: get dressed, get ready for school, eat breakfast, and get to the bus stop on time. It's important to do all of these things, but could you be forgetting something?

God wants us to remember him and thank him. It helps to be thankful toward God at the beginning of the day. Stopping to thank him in the morning gives you peace and joy that can last the whole day.

PRAYER REQUESTS

God, thank you for everything good and right you have blessed us with. Help us to focus more on what we are grateful for, and less on what we don't have. We want to reflect gratitude and contentment in our daily lives and learn to choose thankfulness each day.

Enter his gates with thanksgiving
and his courts with praise;
give thanks to him and praise his name.

PSALM 100:4 NIV

Let's talk!

What are you most grateful for today?

What can you thank God for right now?

How do you ask God for things? Do you complain about what you don't have, or tell him exactly what you want? Sometimes we think of God as our magic guy in the sky who will pay for everything, fix everything, and make sure we have exactly what we want.

God wants us to tell him what we need, what we are afraid of, and how we need help, but he also wants us to tell him when we are happy, thankful, or amazed. He deserves our thanks, so let's tell him how grateful we are today.

PRAISE REPORT

Share recent answers to prayer.

What are you grateful for today?

Make a thankful tree! Draw a simple picture of a tree and have each member of the family write something they are thankful for on each of the branches.

Dear God, you are so good! Thank you for this day. Thank you for our friends and family. Help us to give you thanks in all we say and do. You are the reason for all the blessings in our lives.

DID YOU KNOW?

Choosing a lifestyle of gratitude helps you sleep better, boosts your immune system, and increases your levels of optimism. This means you will have a much better outlook on life as you wake up each morning. And you will feel healthier as well!

Holding On

*You must hold on, so you can do what God
wants and receive what he has promised.*
HEBREWS 10:36 ICB

Do you like swings? How high can you go? What would
happen if you let go of the ropes on the swing? You
would fall! It's important that we hold on because this is
what helps us go higher and stay safe.

The Bible says that we have to hold on to God like this.
That means we keep following him all the days of our
life. He has promised us a life in heaven, so we shouldn't
ever let go of him.

PRAYER REQUESTS

*Lord, thank you for your promises. Thank you that you
have shown us how to be dependable. We want to keep
holding on to you through our whole lives. We can't wait to
receive your reward of eternal life!*

Those who know the LORD trust him,
because he will not leave those
who come to him.

PSALM 9:10 NCV

How do you know that the world is round? How do you know that there are planets in the sky? We have to trust that the scientists who say these things are telling the truth and know a lot of facts about the universe we live in.

We have to trust God in the same way. God is even greater than the smartest scientist in the world. He knows everything. When God says something is true, or gives his people a promise, we can believe him entirely!

Let's talk!

How difficult is it for you to trust people?

How do you know you can trust God?

PRAISE REPORT
Share recent answers to prayer.

What are you grateful for today?

When you open the fridge is there generally food inside? When it rains does your roof keep you dry? When you hurt yourself, are your parents there to help you feel better? Discuss things that you depend on in your daily life. Parents do a pretty good job of taking care of their kids but they aren't perfect. God is our perfect example of dependability.

Dear Jesus, we know we can always trust you. You are the way to eternal life. Help us to come to you when we have questions about our faith or we are afraid of something. We need you.

DID YOU KNOW?

Koalas have special bacteria in their stomach that lets them live off an exclusive diet of highly poisonous eucalyptus leaves. Unfortunately, baby koalas aren't born with this nifty bacterium, so what's a momma to do? Well, she feeds her babies her poop, of course! For the first six months of life, the baby koala is fully dependent on its mom while it lives in her pouch and builds its tolerance for eucalyptus leaves. Aren't you glad you are not a koala?

Lifesaving Wisdom

Getting wisdom is the wisest thing you can do!
And whatever else you do, develop
good judgment.
PROVERBS 4:7 NLT

If you couldn't find a trash can, would you throw your garbage on the ground? If you didn't know the answer to a question at school, would you look at someone else's answer? If you saw someone drop their money, would you pick it up and keep it?

We have to make decisions so many times in one day! The Bible says that we need to get wisdom. When we ask for wisdom, we choose to do the right thing. And we usually know what that is because we know what Jesus would do.

PRAYER REQUESTS

Father God, help us to make good decisions and to be wise in all that we do. Teach us to consider whether what we're thinking about doing is a good or bad idea. We want to act with wisdom, so we trust that you will give that to us.

*Wisdom and money can get
you almost anything,
but only wisdom can save your life.*
ECCLESIASTES 7:12 NLT

Let's talk!

How could wisdom help you make better choices?

What can wisdom get you that money cannot?

A good climbing tree doesn't just pop up overnight. It takes years for any tree to grow strong enough for someone to hang from its branches. Even the biggest trees don't stand a chance against strong winds if it is not planted deep into good soil.

God is the rich soil that we need to plant our roots deep down into. He will give us wisdom as long as we spend our time digging deeper into his Word.

PRAISE REPORT
Share recent answers to prayer.

What are you grateful for today?

Good idea or bad idea? Read aloud the following list, asking your family to shout out, "Good idea!" or "Bad idea!" Feel free to add to the list.

• Make fun of the new kid at school.
• Clean up your room the first time you are asked.
• Take money from mom or dad's wallet without asking.
• Ignore your friend when they are sad because you don't feel like listening to their problems.
• Volunteer to help at a fundraiser that will help a family in need.
• Invite a friend to go to church with you.
• Get revenge on someone who was mean to you.

Dear God, we hear a lot about the benefits of being wise or having wisdom. It's not always something we think we can get easily. But you say you will give it to us if we ask for it. We want more wisdom so we can live better lives for you.

DID YOU KNOW?

King Solomon is often referred to as the wisest man in the Bible. God said he could ask for whatever he wanted and God would give it to him. Most men would probably ask for wealth or long life, but Solomon desired wisdom so that he could rule God's people well. Thanks to his selfless request, the people of Israel experienced one of their most peaceful and prosperous eras. King Solomon's wise decisions made him one of the top ten wealthiest human beings to ever live, with an estimated modern-day annual income in the billions.

Waste of Time

"Don't worry. Don't say, 'What will we eat?' Or,
'What will we drink?' Or, 'What will we wear?'
People who are ungodly run after all those
things. Your Father who is in heaven knows that
you need them. But put God's kingdom first. Do
what he wants you to do. Then all those things
will also be given to you."
MATTHEW 6:31-33 NIRV

If you play board games, you will know that there is a start and a finish to every game. As you play a game, there are things that get in the way of you finishing, like not answering a question right, or having to skip a turn.

What if you spent the whole game worrying about what could go wrong? It wouldn't be a very enjoyable game for you. God says that life is like that. You can't keep worrying about what might go wrong. To enjoy life, you need to trust God and look to the finish line—one day you will get to that treasure!

PRAYER REQUESTS

Jesus, help us keep our eyes and hearts centered on you.
We don't want to worry about all the things that could
happen to us or to others. There are so many things we
cannot control. Help us to be ok with that because we trust
in you.

*"Who of you by worrying can
add a single hour to your life?"*

Luke 12:25 NIV

We often find ourselves thinking too much about the wrong things. We might start to worry about what we look like or about playing a new sport. We might wonder if we will ever be good enough for the school musical or think too much about being well liked by everyone. These kinds of thoughts can make us feel nervous.

Isn't it great when people tell you that everything is going to be okay? They might make you laugh or tell you that you don't need to worry. Good words are good for everyone and they need to be shared!

Let's talk!

What worries can you hand over to God today?

What are some good things you can think about instead of worrying about everything that might go wrong?

PRAISE REPORT

Share recent answers to prayer.

What are you grateful for today?

What is your favorite game to play as a family? Take thirty minutes to play it together tonight.

Dear God, we know that worrying about our problems does not help anything. You are all we need. You will never let us fall. We thank you for that, Jesus. Will you help us to learn to trust you with all our worries?

DID YOU KNOW?

George Muller was a German who moved to England to devote his life to serving God fulltime. His original plan of working with the Jewish society didn't pan out, but soon George and his wife were opening a home for orphan girls. The house was quickly filled and a second one opened, then a third, fourth, and even fifth. George didn't worry about the many needs of the orphanage. In fact, George never even once asked for money. But all the food, clothes, and furniture were donated by people in the community. He felt strongly that God would meet all their needs. He went to prayer alone and witnessed several miraculous provisions. Before his death, George oversaw the care of more than 10,000 orphans in England.